Praise for Global Youth Culture

For anyone who has a heart to reach this global youth culture that is being destroyed all around us I highly recommend that you read Luke Greenwood's book! He speaks with authority and with God's broken heart as he shares principles to communicate the love of Jesus to a whole demographic of people all around the world crying out for answers. Read this book or die!

—David Pierce, founder of Steiger International and the band No Longer Music, author of *Rock Priest* and other titles

I couldn't put this book down. So inspiring and eye opening! Luke shares his life of surrender, obedience and faith, with authentic stories that left me on the edge of my seat. He shows deep understanding of the heart of the Global Youth Culture, what drives us, the root of what we believe and what keeps us going. And Luke knows the source of the answer: spending time at the feet of Jesus and stepping outside the church walls to be salt and light. A must read!

—Sarah Breuel, Revive Europe Director, Evangelism Training Coordinator in IFES Europe, Board of Directors for the Lausanne Movement

In the 1860's, Hudson Taylor traveled the British Isles opening Christians' eyes to the vast mission field of China. More than 150 years later, Luke Greenwood sounds the same clarion call about young adults steeped in urban secular culture. Young people all over the world are "seeking truth in themselves and finding emptiness." Through compelling stories from Sao Paulo to Dresden, Greenwood gives us a glimpse of what Jesus is doing to seek a lost generation. Through innovative evangelism and accessible Bible study in uncommon settings, the Holy Spirit is redeeming global youth and transforming them into a potent missions force. Global Youth Culture is a must read for everyone wanting to pay attention to the move of God in our time.

—**Lindsay Olesberg, National Director of Scripture Engagement, InterVarsity/USA, author of** *The Bible Study Handbook*

᪆

"Luke Greenwood is one of the great global voices regarding millennial evangelism. He is an extraordinary practitioner in this space. He is providing extraordinary thought and leadership to this most urgent conversation."

—**Dr. Mac Pier, Founder, Movement.org, Lausanne Catalyst for Cities**

᪆

"Global youth share an increasingly irreligious worldview shaped by popular artists, musicians, and memes distributed around the world. They also share a hunger for redemption. Luke Greenwood invites us to see where God is at work within the global youth culture and join him there—in "the scene"—to make disciples empowered for Christ's mission. Readers may debate what methods work best where they live, but there's no debating the need and no ignoring this inspiring call to action."

—**Brandon J. O'Brien, director of content development and distribution for Redeemer City to City**

᪆

"I love this book! It's a call to action, a guide to a world we know little about, a powerful demonstration of how God is at work amongst young people today, and a great read. Luke's stories back up the wealth of research and experience he has through Steiger, the pioneering ministry that reaches out to those who are often far beyond the doors of our churches, but whose hearts are longing for the love of Jesus. Luke's wisdom, passion, and spirituality back up the model of ministry he advocates and leave no excuse for the church not to be involved with him and others in this vital contemporary ministry. Read it, enjoy it, and take up the challenge of reaching today's global youth!

—**Dr. Richard Harvey, All Nations Christian College and Senior Researcher, Jews for Jesus**

∽

"Luke Greenwood's personal story and calling will inspire and challenge you to join in a movement of Jesus activists to reach the Global Youth Culture with the love of Christ. Like the apostle Paul, Luke's passion is that "Those who were never told of him – they'll see him! Those who've never heard of him – they'll get the message!" (Romans 15:17-21, MSG). This book boldly declares the need, offers relevant solutions, and provides practical ideas for following in the steps of Jesus to reach a group of people who are largely invisible to the traditional church.

—**Blair T. Carlson, GoodWORD Partnership, formerly International Crusade Director for Billy Graham and Congress Director, Cape Town 2010: The Third Lausanne Congress on World Evangelization**

∽

"Luke Greenwood's message is a timely, much-needed prophetic reminder to all of us followers of Jesus that the days are dark, and yet, never have the opportunities to reach and disciple the Global Youth Culture been any brighter. Luke carries a passionate simplicity for the lost meeting Jesus that always encourages my heart and life."

—**Chad Johnson, Former Director of A&R for Tooth & Nail Records, Founder, Come&Live!**

∽

"Churches are failing to address the topics young people are interested in. Many churches do not even offer youth work anymore or when they offer, many of them find their work irrelevant, making no difference in the youth of today. They see no solution to fix this problem. Therefore, I am totally excited about this new book *Global Youth Culture* on the market praying that it will meet this incredible need of showing who these young people in the global youth culture are and actually showing how easy it is to not only love but engage with them and invite them to follow Jesus. This book serves as an eye-opener to this young generation and should be read by all leaders responsible in churches and in society. I love what Luke Greenwood and Steiger International accomplish and highly respect that they practice what they teach. Let's not accept for another generation to be lost for the Kingdom of God! There is no time for losing hearts but to join this revolution!"

—Evi Rodemann, MA in European Mission, Chair of Lausanne YLGen Groups & Gatherings, Cheerleader of the next generation!

≪⟨

"We live in confusing and challenging times. This is a solid book with deep insight into what is actually happening with a modern global generation. It helped me to identify the cultural gap between society and Christianity and at the same time find mature and efficient ways to bridge this gap and communicate truth relevantly. It was very helpful in my work as I seek to effectively reach a secularized global youth culture."

—Misha Nokrashvili, lead singer for Nuteki, leader of Steiger Belarus

≪⟨

"Many people may feel discouraged and concerned as they look out at the global youth culture of our generation. However, Luke helps us to see this is an opportunity rather than just a challenge and shows the power of the gospel to bring hope, healing, and transformation into some of the darkest and most unlikely contexts. Read this book and you will be reminded afresh at the wonder of the gospel and its relevance for every age and generation. Packed with exciting stories of faith filled adventures, it will encourage, excite, and equip you to reach young people for Jesus."

—Michael Ots, Author, Evangelist and Apologist

≪⟨

"An urgent call to understand and engage with globalised youth culture, increasingly shaped by secular humanism and modern technology. Out of the box, visionary, passionate, challenging."

—Lindsay Brown, former International Director of the Lausanne Movement and IFES

∽

"Luke is eminently qualified to rally his readers toward reaching the youth of the globe, having personally served on the front lines of evangelism since his call into ministry as a teenager. His book will inspire you with personal stories, conversations, and powerful insights into global youth culture. But Luke is more than just an insightful commentator; his passion for Christ, confidence in the gospel, and grounding in God's Word will equip you to reach this next generation without compromise. I highly recommend his book to anyone who cares about one of the greatest missions' challenges facing the church today – reaching the global youth culture for Christ."

—Dave Patty, founder and president of Josiah Venture

∽

"This book will challenge and inspire you to reach this generation. Many times we wait to see if people become open to God, but this book shows us that God is ready to reach into the empty spaces of people's lives right now. Luke acutely describes the mindset of the current youth and equips you to walk out your life filled with Jesus and display the genuine gospel in this very opportune time for them to hear it. I love Luke's heart and dedication to showing people from all walks of life who the true Jesus really is, his passion will truly inspire you."

—Ben Fitzgerald, Leader of Awakening Europe

Global Youth Culture

Global Youth Culture

The Spiritual Hunger of the Largest
Unreached Culture Today

Luke Greenwood

Global Youth Culture

Copyright © 2019 by Luke Greenwood

Published and distributed by Steiger International.

Paperback ISBN: 978-1-912149-33-9
eBook ISBN: 978-1-912149-34-6

Cover design by: Derek Thornton at Notch Design (www.notchdesign.com)

Printed in the United States of America

Contents

FOREWORD 14

ACKNOWLEDGMENTS 16

INTRODUCTION 18

UNHAPPY, UNLOVED AND OUT OF CONTROL 21

THE CALLING 27
    SURRENDER 29
    CALLING OR AMBITION? 32
    A MISSION CALLED STEIGER 34

THE LARGEST UNREACHED CULTURE TODAY 38
    PLAGUE SQUARE 39
    WE ARE CONNECTED 42
    WE ARE CONSUMERS 48

WHAT YOU BELIEVE MATTERS 52
    TODAY'S GLOBAL WORLDVIEW 54
    DESPERATE...56
    ARROGANT 58
    PRETTY . . . PRETTY VACANT 60

LOST 62
    THE FEAR 63
    THE HUNGER 64
    THE DISSATISFACTION 66
    THE EMPTINESS 68

THE SOURCE OF HOPE 73
    SEEK GOD 75
    SEEK GOD WITH YOUR WIFE (OR HUSBAND IF YOU'RE A GIRL) 78
    SEEK GOD FOR VISION AND POWER 82

KNOW THE SCENE **86**

STEP OUTSIDE THE CHURCH WALLS 89
JESUS KNEW THE SCENE 93
THE ART THAT JESUS MASTERED 96
BECOMING ALL THINGS TO THE SCENE 100
MANIFESTE 102
GO TO THEM 104

SPEAK THE TRUTH **108**

MURMANSK 110
LIFTING UP THE CROSS OUTSIDE THE CHURCH 112
POWERFUL TRUTH 114
SUBVERSIVE TRUTH 118
PROVOCATIVE TRUTH 121
CLEAR TRUTH 125

STAY TOGETHER **130**

JESUS THE DISCIPLE MAKER 134
BARNABAS THE DISCIPLE MAKER 136
BIBLE 137
COMMUNITY 142

JOIN THE REVOLUTION **148**

STEIGER'S VALUES 152
GET INVOLVED 154
FIGHTING THE GOOD FIGHT 156
SOMETHING WORTH MORE THAN LIFE ITSELF 161

APPENDIX **165**

INFORMAL BIBLE STUDY GUIDE 165
GETTING STARTED 170
BIBLE 172
COMMUNITY 174
BIBLE STUDY MEETINGS 177
GENERAL OUTLINE OF THE MEETING 181
TOPICAL MEETINGS 183
EVENT 185
BAPTISM 186
SAMPLE BIBLE STUDIES 188

THE JESUS REVOLUTION PT1 188
THE JESUS REVOLUTION PT2 191
SOMETHING WORTH LIVING FOR 194
GOD'S BROKEN HEART 196

ABOUT STEIGER 198

ABOUT THE AUTHOR 200

NOTES 203

Foreword

By Brian Welch

On August 27, 2017, my band Korn was playing an enormous music festival in the UK called the Leeds Festival with Major Lazer and headliner Eminem; it was an odd combination but a very fun lineup nonetheless. Luke Greenwood, who I had met through Steiger International, and some of his friends helped gather a load of Korn fans at the festival after our set.

Since I hadn't attempted to gather fans at any other mainstream festival that tour, I really didn't know what to expect. Usually festivals that gigantic are too hectic and have so many things going on that I don't even try to put on a spiritual gathering with Korn fans like I do at our headlining concerts.

If there is one thing I've learned from traveling the globe multiple times over, it's that having passionate people around you is an essential ingredient with nontraditional ministry outreach. And Luke ended up being that passionate friend I needed that day at Leeds Festival. Luke and some brothers and sisters from Steiger organized an amazing tent meeting with Korn fans and when I had walked into the tent to tell my story to these amazing youth, I was shocked to see the tent full of hungry souls.

We saw many youths weep that day as we shared the story of the Godman who is the very definition of Hope: Jesus Christ. Most of the crowd responded to the message and came forward as we gave out Bibles and prayed for people. One girl who came forward shared her heartbreaking story with us, as she revealed scars from self-harming up both arms. "I got out of a psychiatric unit just to come and see the Korn show", she explained. "You have no idea how much this message meant to me". We told her about God's love for her and prayed that she would be free and know the peace of Jesus.

I started getting involved with the Steiger guys around 2016, coming on their *Provoke & Inspire* podcast, and since then they have helped organize meetings like this all around the world, including South America, the USA, Germany, Poland, Switzerland, Ukraine and even Japan. We've seen people open up to Jesus everywhere.

One of the reasons I recognize the burden and passion in Luke Greenwood and Steiger for the youth, is because I have it burned into my soul as well. All of us long for the key to unlock the souls of the youth in the world. We yearn for the world's youth to put aside what the media has said about Christianity and our only desire is to lead them not to the Christian religion but to Jesus Himself. Jesus is real. He is alive. And the young generation of the world need Jesus to manifest Himself to them in a fresh, supernatural way.

In *Global Youth Culture* Luke Greenwood writes about the mission to do whatever it takes to impact the Global Youth Culture for Jesus. I am convinced that absolutely nothing is going to stop Luke and Steiger Ministries from fighting to achieve this goal.

As you read this book ask yourself *how am I going to be involved?*

Acknowledgments

The greatest present Jesus gave me on this earth is my beautiful family, Ania, Daniel and Sara. Thank you for the support, respect, joy, fun, and love I have in you. Love you guys!

My parents, Phil and Jan, were my first disciplers and mentors. They spurred me on to do whatever God called me to do, and continue to be a source of wisdom and encouragement until today. Thank you!

Ania and I are blessed to have various churches around the world who are our family and who have invested in us and cared for us at different stages of our lives. Cheam Baptist Church are our sending church and have walked with us for over ten years. Thank you CBC! Pipe and Katia and Golgota church in Curitiba, Sandro and Mara and Projeto 242 family in São Paulo, The Rock in Wroclaw, thank you for years of being able to serve Jesus together!

I want to thank our Steiger family all around the world! You guys are who keep us going strong for Jesus, your passion inspires us, your love holds us up. I thank David and Jodi Pierce, you guys fanned the flame that Jesus put in my heart and taught me how to reach the Global Youth Culture! Aaron Pierce, thank you for being a friend and "partner in crime" as we've built this mission up together!

Thank you Brian Welch, Jorge Cumplido (Cocke), Moah, Flavia and Guarulhos gang, No Longer Music, Bruno Colisse and Alegorica, Manifeste team, Dudi, Dalila, Angelo, Aline and Steiger São Paulo team, Steiger Wroclaw team, Stephan Maag, Angela and Steiger Union

(Russian-speaking world) for the great adventures we have lived together and the many more to come.

Greetings to my brothers in The Unrest. The riot has only just begun!

I want to thank Lindsay Olesberg, Richard Harvey, Luciana Kim and Maureen Hurst for your important input along the way as this book has been in the making. Geoffrey Stone thank you for taking this book to the next level and turning it into something people can actually read :-) Derek Thornton thank you for making the book look great!

Introduction

We are the global generation. Urbanised and connected, we believe in freedom, equality, democracy, and justice. We are free and in control. We are tech savvy, artists and activists. We love image, beauty and quality. We are open-minded, spiritual, tolerant, and diverse. We want change and we want more. We want everything now, but really, we don't know what we want.

We have never been so close and at the same time so far from each other, never before so confused by life, its meaning, and its purpose. We have been bombarded by the entertainment industry, pop culture, and economic strategies. We've been told to believe anything, accept everything, and trust no one. We believe we can buy our identities. We treat people like we treat stuff. We want to fight, but we don't know what to fight for. We feel empty, numb, and confused. We've stepped below the line of despair, we have no hope, and we don't know what to believe anymore. We are the Global Youth Culture, and this is our cry.

The current urban generation, connected by consumerism, social media, and the entertainment industry forms the largest global culture to ever exist. It spans from Europe to South America, from Asia to the

Middle East, holding the same values, listening to the same music, watching the same movies, and sharing the same posts.

This global culture is largely influenced by one predominant worldview: secular humanism. God is dead and we are at the centre. In this relativistic culture we are god, and consumerism is our religion. This is a generation that does not look to the church for answers, as it believes it to be a dead and empty tradition of the past. Either there is no God, or if He is there, He doesn't really interfere with our lives.

But God is on a mission and His heart is broken for this lost generation. The message of His love—the gospel—is for everyone, and it is not right that young people today don't get to hear it because we're not making it accessible to them.

According to a 2014 survey by the Pew Research Centre, there are now approximately 56 million religiously unaffiliated Americans.[1] A similar study entitled "Europe's Young Adults and Religion," by British professor of theology and sociology of religion Stephen Bullivant, shows an even more drastic reality. In the Czech Republic, 91 percent of young adults categorised themselves as religiously unaffiliated, while in the UK, France, Belgium, Spain, and the Netherlands between 56 percent and 60 percent said they never go to church and between 63 percent and 66 percent said they never pray. According to Bullivant, many young Europeans "will have been baptised and then never darken the door of a church again. Cultural religious identities just aren't being passed on from parents to children. It just washes straight off them".[2]

They don't come to us, so we need to go to them. As Jesus' church, we need to realise the necessary changes in mind-set and lifestyle, and the need for a paradigm shift in missions.

This is our manifesto. To challenge the status quo of the secular humanistic worldview and unmask its oppressive nature. To lift up the Cross outside the church and see the message of a loving God revealed in Jesus, infused in this globalised culture. To see this generation find hope and purpose again as it meets the Creator. And through this, to radically and eternally change the world.

My hope in writing this book is to raise awareness of the spiritual hunger of this Global Youth Culture and spark a mission movement to preach the Gospel in urban centres all over the world.

1

Unhappy, Unloved and Out of Control

In 2008, an edition of *Time* magazine focused on the plight of British young people. The front cover showed a typical, angry-looking "hoodie" with the headline "Unhappy, Unloved and Out of Control". The main article of this edition accurately described a lot of what we were seeing around us:

> The boys and girls who casually pick fights, have sex and keep the emergency services fully occupied are often fuelled by cheap booze. British youngsters drink their Continental European counterparts under the table… British kids were also involved more frequently in fights… They are more likely to try drugs or to start smoking young. English girls are the most sexually active in Europe. More of them are having sex aged 15 or younger, and more than 15% fail to use contraception when they do - which means that Britain has high rates of both teen pregnancy and sexually transmitted diseases.[1]

The article went on to say that a 2007 Unicef research of child well-being in twenty-one industrialised countries put the UK at the bottom of the list.

My wife, Ania, and I were living in the UK then, spending time with our home church that supports us as missionaries. This article spoke deeply to me as we had gotten to know first-hand the reality of many young people in the UK – lives often full of pain, lostness, and confusion. There was a vast generation gap, and young people with no purpose were living empty, materialistic lifestyles with nothing much to do but hang around and drink in the parks and high streets.

Once, I remember Ania asking a fifteen-year-old girl what she wanted to do with her life and what her dreams were. She said she wanted to get pregnant. "Why?" Ania asked.

"So that I can get support from social services. They give single mum's a nice flat and an allowance".

We decided to take action. We announced at a Sunday morning service that we were hosting a prayer meeting for anyone who wanted to help us reach young people in our neighbourhood. Later that week as some of our friends and other church members started to trickle into the front room of our flat in Sutton, in Southwest London, I wondered what we were doing. We weren't exactly a cutting-edge, dynamic youth team. Some of our team were so shy they didn't even like talking to *us*, and we were their friends! We had a librarian, a car salesman, and Grandma Pat who was seventy-nine year's old, full of energy, and with a constant smile on her face. None of us had much experience with youth work, but we all had willing hearts. We spent a month in prayer trying to discern what we should do to reach the youth in our neighbourhood. Finally, we agreed we would organise a party in a café next to the church.

We made some cool-looking flyers and went to the high street (main shopping district) to invite people. I came up to a group of "hoodies" (teens with hoods over their faces who like football, girls, drinking, and beating each other up). I told them about the party as I handed out the flyers. They took the invitations and then proceed to rip them up, and spit on them, and then started hurling abuse at me. "You're one of those f**** Christians!" I have no idea how they knew as the flyer said nothing about it being a Christian event.

When we met with the team, I told them I didn't think anyone would come. And I was right. That Saturday, we sat in the café looking at each other, wondering what to do. So, we prayed, "God, we don't know how to reach these guys. Please bring them to our café, so we can tell them about you".

During the following week, I got a message from one of the church members saying kids in her school were all talking about a cool new café that had opened up, and she was wondering if it was our café. To this day, I don't know how to explain what happened, but the following Saturday, when we opened the café, there were lines of people waiting to get in. Maybe a few trendsetters decided they were coming, and everyone else just followed, I don't know.

The place was packed, the music was pulsing, and I was worried. I thought to myself, "When I gave them flyers, they almost punched me! If I try speaking about Jesus here tonight, they might kill me!" So I prayed, "God I know I said we'd tell them about you, but I'm sure you understand the risks here, and that it's probably not a good idea to preach at them, right?" Then I felt like God answered, "You asked me to fill the place, so now preach!"

I got up on a table and shouted, "Hello everybody! Thank you for coming to our new café! We want you all to know that you are very welcome here, and that we love having you! I also wanted to tell you that God loves you!" Of course, at this point, the abuse started: "Shut up, you idiot! Don't start with the God stuff!" (Well, that's not *exactly* what they said. They used more explicit vocabulary.) I decided to keep going, "Right, listen up! If anyone here would like to hear me reading the Bible, I will be in a room upstairs. You can stay here and continue enjoying the party, or you can follow me upstairs". At this point, I bolted up the stairs and collapsed on a couch, thinking to myself, "Well, I did what I could. I'll wait here awhile, then head home with a clean conscience".

To my shock and despair, people started coming up the stairs. They filled the chairs set out in the little room and more kept on coming. They sat on the floor, and soon the room was packed. Others stood in the corridor, peering through the doorway to see inside. I thought to myself, "What do these guys want from me?! When I preach, they yell at me! I give them a good opportunity to chill downstairs, but no, they want to mock me more!"

To be honest I hadn't really prepared anything, as I was certain no one would want to come to hear me read from the Bible! I mean, who would want to listen to that? So I improvised. I opened to the passage where Jesus calms the storm and began to read. When I finished, I explained that the same Jesus who calmed that storm was alive and was in the room with us and that He had the same power today.

The room was silent. I couldn't believe they were listening. Then the questions started coming: "But how can you really believe this?" "At school we're taught there is no God and that we all came from the Big Bang". "My parents told me church is a bunch of lies". Suddenly our shy team was surrounded by young guys and girls curiously asking questions. We tried answering as best we could and found that behind all that aggression, they were honestly curious and seriously thirsty for truth. They had never had the chance to sit and talk to someone about Jesus like this, and they were fascinated by it.

Grandma Pat had never made so much tea and hot chocolate in her life. And she loved it. Every Saturday she was the first to arrive and one of the last to leave. She'd greet everyone with a hug and called them "dear". Even the most hardened guys couldn't help but love her. "Grandma Pat!" they all called her, and she would sit and talk to them all night. She became quite the celebrity in our area. Young people greeted her at every corner when she was out doing her shopping down Sutton high street. And it wasn't only her. Our whole team was revolutionised by what God was doing through this simple step of faith.

It became a weekly event at Point Night Café, as we called it. Every Saturday, some of the guys who had been the rowdiest at the beginning were the ones coming up and asking, "When is the Bible study starting tonight?" They even brought notebooks full of questions they had thought of at school during the week.

I'll never forget this one guy, Sam. He had been one of the angry mob leaders on that first night, but soon he was a regular at the upstairs Bible study. One Saturday, he came to me and said, "Mate, something really weird happened to me this week". "What's up Sam?" "I had this urge to pray, so I did! And I feel like God listened. I feel like He accepted me as I am".

My generation has been brought up confused by relativism and secularism. Bombarded by the materialistic entertainment industry, we've been sold an empty dream. But they are thirsty for truth. When they have the opportunity to meet the real Jesus, rather than slogans and superficial answers to questions they've never asked, they are ready and willing to drop it all and follow Him.

This globalised and secularised youth culture needs a new missionary movement led by bold and authentic followers of Jesus who are passionate about their faith and willing to take the risks to live out that faith in their lives today.

Those meetings at Point Night Cafe lasted about two years. Grandma Pat didn't want to stop. In her eighties she joined a London-based group called the Street Pastors and started going to the clubbing areas to talk and pray with people coming out of the clubs in the early hours of the morning. Another couple that had been on our team went to Hong Kong as missionaries to work with renowned missionary Jackie Pullinger and her St. Stephen's Society.

You don't have to be great in human eyes, you don't have to be hip, and you don't have to have a theology degree to make a difference. You just need a heart surrendered to God's calling.

2

The Calling

When I was fifteen, I had a band. We had big dreams of being rock stars for Jesus. The plan was to become really famous and then we would tell everyone about Jesus. As we lived in the middle of nowhere in São Paulo, Brazil, we believed we were one of, if not the first, Christian, progressive heavy metal bands in the world.

I somehow managed to wear tight black leather trousers and a matching *Matrix*-style overcoat in the Brazilian heat, and I developed a technique of playing drums and swinging my hair in circles at the same time.

You might be surprised to hear my missionary parents were quite understanding. Maybe it was because my dad spent his youth listening to Deep Purple and met my mum at a Bible study as she rolled up on a motorbike. The story goes that my dad walked over to my mum, who had just parked her bike in a forbidden spot. He said, "Look here, mate, you can't park there". My mum proceeded to pull off her helmet and her long, blond, curly hair cascaded down in true Hollywood style, leaving my dad stuttering. He was unable to find the courage to ask her out for the next twelve months.

Ten years into their marriage, my parents felt called to leave my dad's safe office job in a petrol company and semi-detached house in a middle-class Southwest London borough, to be missionaries in Brazil. So in 1992, with me (age eight) and my two sisters (four and six), they moved to a small flat in the interior of São Paulo, the next coastal state south of Rio de Janeiro.

Anyway, back to the band. After our first two years of great success, playing at least one gig in a local theatre (which made the local newspaper!), our big plans were put on hold while I attended university in the larger city of Curitiba south of São Paulo. In 2001, I moved to Curitiba. A friend had told me it was heavy metal city. There were various CD shops entirely dedicated to metal, and there were bars with live gigs every weekend. I was pretty excited, being out of my parent's house and starting my quite precocious independent life at only seventeen.

At one of the first gigs I went to I discovered the members of the band playing were Christians. Another Christian heavy metal band? I was shocked. Turns out others had thought of the missionary band idea before me. They told me about a church they were planting to reach alternative young people in the city.

The very next Sunday I turned up to check it out. It was a narrow building on a steep road in a very dodgy part of town. It was known to be one of the main drug-dealing and prostitution areas. The first thing I noticed was the entire front of the building, including the tall window panes, was painted in thick black paint. The entrance was a tall twisted metal gate and one of the church members was standing guard. He had fiery red hair held back with a Guns N' Roses bandana and was entirely clad in black leather. To add to his intimidating ensemble, Kiss, as he was known, was holding back his rottweiler Aslan with a huge thick chain.

Golgota church was something I'd never imagined could exist, but I fit straight in and spent the next few years growing fast in my faith. The church was planted by an awesome couple – Volmir, better known as Pastor Pipe, and Katia. I was stretched as I got involved helping the small church-planting team lead Bible studies and one-on-one discipleship with the rapidly growing community of young people coming from various subcultures: punk, metal, hippie, rave, emo, and others. Basically, anyone coming to Jesus who didn't fit into a traditional church setting seemed to end up coming through our doors.

My ambitious plan for a missionary metal band suddenly didn't seem that original. In our church, there were more bands than people. Yet, despite my own plans and ideas, there was a God-given desire growing inside me. I wanted to see my friends, and many other young people who I knew would never walk into a church, discover that Jesus is real and that church isn't about a building or a set of rules.

Surrender

I longed to find new ways of communicating the truth and reality of Jesus to my generation, that they might have the same privilege of knowing God. But my pride, my rock star complex, was in the way.

In that first year in Curitiba, I moved into a flat with two other guys, just down the road from our church. As I said before, this was an area heavy with prostitution and drug trafficking. There were kids as young as seven smoking crack cocaine and sleeping on my doorstep.

Every morning on my way to university I'd walk by girls selling their bodies on street corners and crack-crazed kids searching for cans in the rubbish. As I passed by I would pray, "God please change this situation. Someone has to do something about this".

One day I felt like He answered: "You do something about it".

"But God I don't know how to talk to prostitutes and drug addicts. I'm going to be a rock star and tell multitudes of people about you".

I couldn't get it out of my head, I felt like God was telling me to do something totally contrary to my plan and what I thought made sense. So one morning I got up, made a flask of coffee, and decided to offer it to the people on the street in an effort to show I cared and to talk to them. I went down to the corner and offered a cup of coffee to a tall guy dressed in a mini skirt. The transvestite looked at me suspiciously. "I know why you've come here," he said. You want to complain about the noise and the mess on your street, with us running our business out here all night".

"No, I honestly just wanted to offer you coffee. This might sound strange, but I walk by here each day. I pray for you, and I felt like God told me to come and tell you that He cares". It was as if a weight was lifted from his shoulders. He thanked me, accepted the coffee, and started opening up about his life. I was able to pray with him and give him a pocket version of the Gospel of Luke.

Around that time I went to a missions conference. There were so many great people doing amazing things for God all over the world. I started comparing myself to these cool missionaries, thinking about all the great things I might do one day. I started to feel overwhelmed, so I stepped outside and sat on a bench. I opened my Bible and suddenly had a deep sense God wanted to show me something. I randomly turned to Psalm 131:

> My heart is not proud, Lord,
>
>> my eyes are not haughty;
>
> I do not concern myself with great matters
>
>> or things too wonderful for me.
>
> But I have calmed and quieted myself,
>
>> I am like a weaned child with its mother;
>
>> like a weaned child I am content.

I was convicted of my proud heart. There were dreams God had put in me, but often it would get mixed up and entangled with a proud ambition, and a desire to be recognised. I repented.

But God didn't leave it there. He wanted me to act on it. First, I felt like He was urging me, in the middle of a meeting with all those missionaries I had just met, to get up and confess my proud ambition and desire for recognition. So, trembling, I went forward and shared. I don't expect it meant much to anyone else in the room, but God was doing something in my heart.

When I got home, I felt God's calling on me. I quit the band I was in at the time (by that point I had already been part of a few different bands in Golgota church), gave my drum kit to the church, and dedicated myself to sharing God's love with people on my own doorstep. Soon some friends from church joined me and there were a bunch of us reaching prostitutes and drug addicts all over the centre of Curitiba.

God's plan is so much better than ours. Years later I did end up touring around the world with a band, but by then my heart was changed. I really didn't care anymore about being in a band or playing drums. All I cared about was seeing people come to Jesus. Just as I'd seen Him move powerfully on the streets in Curitiba, I wanted to see people meet Him in each show we played. More on that later.

*
**

The first thing we need to do to see God's calling happen in our lives is surrender. This is huge in our "selfie" culture. It means to take a radical stand against the flow of the culture. And that is exactly what is needed if we're to reach this generation for Jesus. There is no perfect strategy or great formula. We need God's power. And to see God's power we have to surrender.

Calling or Ambition?

I'd decided early on that I didn't want to depend financially on my parents. I had a great relationship with them (although I probably should have called home more often), but it just seemed right to me that I had to grow up and learn to look after myself. So I got a job teaching English. I also continued the street ministry through the four years I lived in Curitiba. This meant that I was at university in the mornings, teaching English lessons in the afternoons, and spending most evenings on the streets talking to drug addicts, prostitutes, and homeless people. Those were very intense years; I definitely didn't get bored. It also meant I often stayed out until one or two in the morning and then got up early for classes. Once I spent so much time out in the cold Curitiba nights with our homeless friends that I caught pneumonia and had to spend a week in the hospital.

Our prayer times as a team before going out to the streets were often intense spiritual battles. It was literally a fight to bring Jesus to such dark parts of the city. At times I felt tired, lonely, and out of my depth. But there was something beyond myself that was driving me. The sense of God's calling gave me all the energy I needed to face the good times and the hard times. I would never have been able to do this if it were just my own plans and ambition. To serve God and go where He asked, I had to know it was a calling and not just my own ambition.

> It is easier to serve or work for God without a vision and without a call, because then you are not bothered by what he requires. Common sense, covered with a layer of Christian emotion, becomes your guide. You may be more prosperous and successful from the world's perspective, and will have more leisure time, if you never acknowledge the call of God. But once you receive a commission from Jesus Christ, the memory of what God asks of you will always be there to prod you on to do His will. You will no longer be able to work for Him on the basis of common sense. (Oswald Chambers, *My Utmost for His Highest*)

I believe Jesus has a commission for anyone who asks, What do you want me to do? So the question isn't Am I called? but What am I called to do? The problem is, sometimes we're so busy doing good things, we don't really ask Him what He would have us do.

In Acts we read about the apostle Paul and the radical calling he received from Jesus to go to the Gentiles. He poured out his life for them and did it with joy. He compared his calling to an athlete in training and a race that he runs to win. He gave everything he had to fulfil his calling: "Even if I am being poured out as a drink offering on the sacrifice and service coming from your faith, I am glad and rejoice with you all" (Philippians 2:17).

When we surrender to Him and receive that commission, God's calling is overwhelmingly powerful and consuming. It is beyond us and out of our control. You just keep taking steps of obedience, often without really knowing what you're doing. Later you look back amazed at God's awesome plan.

When we're called by God, we work hard, give our best, live to a higher standard, and pour ourselves out without even thinking of it. It's not out of legalism or pressure; it just comes naturally to a soul completely surrendered to the King.

A Mission Called Steiger

After letting go of the rock star complex, I started praying for a new vision. Joining my experience reaching disenfranchised young people with Golgota church and my upbringing in the missionary world, I started to envision a new mission organisation that could reach young people who wouldn't walk into a church. Old habits die hard, so I set myself a new ambitious plan: If I wasn't going to have the first Christian rock band, I would found the first mission organisation to reach the alternative youth culture.

I started praying that God would lead me to other people around the world who shared this vision. And I didn't have to wait long because that same week, two girls from Germany turned up at our church and told me about a band called No Longer Music. It was made up of missionaries from all over the world who would be performing in São Paulo city on the weekend. Speaking in broken Portuguese, they gave me the location of the show, and I dashed home to pack a bag.

I was on the next bus – a six-hour ride – to São Paulo. I was so excited. I felt like God was answering my prayers and leading me to something new. Arriving at the chaotic São Paulo bus station, I discovered that the gig was actually happening in another town on the outskirts of the city. By the time I got another bus and made it to the small town of Arujá, it was almost midnight. The bus driver dropped me off near a sign on a dirt road in the middle of nowhere and said, "Walk that way," pointing into the darkness beyond the dirt track.

"What am I doing," I thought. I was seventeen years old, walking along a dirt road in the middle of the night, hardly able to see my own feet. As I continued, my prayers grew in intensity. "God, please help me find this band. I don't want to sleep out here in the woods," I pleaded. Suddenly, I heard the sound of distorted guitars in the distance, and as I followed them, I came to a clearing.

It looked like a typical church retreat centre, but the people there definitely didn't look like church people. Everyone was dressed in black with chains and piercings everywhere. One guy was wearing a gas mask—not for health reasons but as a fashion statement. I found out later that I had just walked into a "meet the band" weekend at the end of No Longer Music's tour of the São Paulo goth scene. These were young people who had just come to know Jesus in goth clubs like Madam Satan, Deja Vu, and the Bloody Covenant Bar, and they'd come here to understand more about the message.

I watched No Longer Music's show for the first time. They portrayed Jesus' death on the Cross and His resurrection, and I saw how people responded to the clear gospel message presented. I knew at that moment that this was what God was calling me to dedicate my life to. I'd come to the right place, and God was answering my prayers.

The next day, I met with David Pierce, the lead singer and founder of No Longer Music. I told him all about my ambitious dream to start a mission organisation to reach young people. David patiently listened to this probably quite annoying seventeen-year-old and then said, "Have you ever heard of Steiger?"

"No," I responded.

"Well, it's basically the mission organisation you're describing. Maybe God is calling you to start a new mission or maybe he's calling you to join us. If you want to be part of Steiger, you should come to our gathering next month".

Amazed at God's awesome plan and direction, I immediately replied, "Sure, I'll come! Where will it be?"

"Poland".

In the early 2000s, Steiger was more a movement than an organisation. It all started in the early eighties with David and Jodi Pierce and No Longer Music in Amsterdam.[1] They inspired a lot of people around the world and began this movement of friends and partners who were all focused on sharing Jesus with young people outside the church. There was stuff happening in Germany, Poland, the USA, Brazil, and other countries.

David once explained God's call to me like this. It's like you're this rat who's been flushed down a drain pipe. You have two options: either you go down scratching and squealing, or you embrace it and enjoy the ride. Either way, you're going down. The fact is, God's calling is overwhelmingly powerful and consuming. When He calls us, our part is to simply obey.

When I got home, I called my mother and said, "Mum, I need to go to Poland".

"Why?" she asked.

"I'm going to join a mission organisation called Steiger".

"Okay. Be safe and don't forget to call".

So I sold some of my stuff, bought a ticket, and was on my way to the Slot Art Festival and Steiger gathering in Poland. I got lost a few times on that trip too but eventually made it. God was answering my prayers, and I was willing to do whatever it took to be a part of what He was doing.

3

The Largest Unreached Culture Today

While still going through a four-year university degree in Curitiba, I got increasingly involved in the work of Steiger in Brazil and around the world. Initially it was things like translating David Pierce when he was preaching and helping organise tours for No Longer Music (known as NLM) in Brazil.

Then, one time in 2004, in a car with David and Sandro Baggio, who is responsible for first bringing NLM and Steiger to Brazil, David said, "I need a new drummer".

"Luke is a drummer!" Sandro spontaneously responded. From that day on David introduced me in every church meeting we went to as his new drummer. I tried explaining that I'd given up drumming years ago, but it was no use. Next thing I knew I was flying to Germany for rehearsals and joining NLM to tour the world and share Jesus.

No Longer Music's purpose was to lift up the Cross in the secular scene. There were plenty of Christian bands around playing good music for Christians, and there were bands of Christians playing in the secular music scene, but more like secret agents undercover. NLM didn't play in churches or Christian festivals. We played in secular clubs and festivals and central squares. But we were far from being undercover secret agents.

NLM has played many different music styles over the years, changing with the times, but one thing remained the same: a dramatisation of a modern-day crucifixion and resurrection of Jesus. Yet probably what has marked NLM the most is the incredible impact the power of the gospel has had on crowds all over the world in places where it is never usually preached. Thousands of people have responded to the good news through this concert over the last thirty years. On every tour I've been on, I've met people saying they first met Jesus through an NLM concert and now were pastors or church planters in some part of the world.

Plague Square

Tour was pretty insane back then. We got sent a list of places where we would play and songs we should learn. I then had to book all my air tickets and hope we'd all meet up somehow in each place and know the songs well enough to hit the road after a week of intense rehearsals.

In 2007, we arrived in Helsinki, Finland, greeted by Kakkerlak ("cockroach" in Dutch) at the airport. He was a Polish Steiger missionary serving in Finland, to whom David for some reason gave a Dutch nickname. He told us he'd arranged a great concert at the Helsinki Festival's Night of the Arts, in a place called Ruttopuisto, which means "plague park," apparently because it used to be a graveyard.

I'd never seen so much cutting-edge alternative fashion in one place. Plague Park was packed, and most kids were already drunk and high by seven p.m. A couple of girls came up to me and asked if lesbians were allowed to come to our concert. I said "of course, bring them all!" And from what I could tell they did.

Some of us decided to walk around and talk to people. We approached one group and asked them what they were expecting from the concert. They didn't know we were with the band, so they were quite honest with us, "We heard there's going to be a really bad band playing here tonight. They're f****** Christians!"

A sweet looking girl with a flat cap and white cut-up leggings added, "I'm an atheist by the way".

"What do you guys have against Christianity?" I asked.

"It's outdated," explained another guy, casually leaning against a gravestone. "I don't think we need any religion. We just need love".

"Yeah!" his friend added. "God doesn't exist, so Christian rock bands shouldn't exist either".

Trying not to let it get to me, I asked, "So what do you guys believe in? What's the purpose of life for you?"

A pale-skinned dude with a tall black mohawk and leather overcoat held his beer bottle up and explained, "I get up, eat breakfast, go to work, and then go for a beer".

A girl to the side, with deep black hair and pink highlights interrupted, "There is no purpose!" Her boyfriend laughed and licked her ear.

As I walked back to the stage area, stepping over streams of urine and broken bottles, I tried to imagine how this crowd would react to our show. When I reached the door to the trailer where our band was meeting to pray, there was a tall punk urinating against the door.

When I stepped inside, the team was asking God to give them His heart for the people there that night. In reality, though, I didn't feel like being there at all, and certainly didn't feel very sympathetic to the punk defiling our door outside. But as I stood there praying, I realised God didn't see a fashionable and intimidating audience outside. He saw his children wasting themselves away on drugs and alcohol, lost and confused. His heart was broken for them. Tears started rolling down my face, and I asked God to help me show them that He was real and cared about them.

As the concert began around four hundred people gathered in front of the stage. After the crucifixion and resurrection scene, David ended by giving a straight message and inviting people to meet Jesus. The atmosphere had completely changed. People suddenly seemed really open, and God's presence was palpable. A group gathered around us as we stepped off the stage and David invited them to pray. I got goose bumps as various concertgoers joined in, repeating the prayer out loud at the top of their voices.

One guy I met seemed totally blown away by the fact I was talking to him about God. He described various situations in his life in which he realised God was speaking to him. The reality was hitting home that God really did exist and cared about him. He told me he didn't want to become some "religious guy" but that he wanted to know more about Jesus. I encouraged him to pray and read his Bible. After exchanging emails, I left him to think.

We Are Connected

I'd had very similar conversations about faith, God, and the purpose of life with my friends back home at university, and with many people in all the countries where we toured: Germany, Poland, Iceland, USA, Brazil, Chile, and places in Asia and the Middle East, like Kyrgyzstan, Turkey, and Lebanon. Everywhere we went we found a similar reality. You can be in Tokyo, Beirut, London, New York, or São Paulo, and young people share similar values, mindsets, and lifestyles. We're all buying the same technology, wearing the same T-shirts, listening to the same music, watching the same movies, and sharing it all on Facebook and Instagram.

When we toured Beirut, Lebanon, we connected with a thriving rock music scene and played in a festival with bands from around the city. At one point, the organiser told us that a bus of people from the Hezbollah area of town had arrived and that the next band to play was a Hezbollah thrash metal band. I'd never imagined that combination of words together. After the show, I spent time with three guys from this band at a café across the street. I asked them about their faith. They explained that their ID cards said they were Muslim and their parents were Muslim, but they were not. They considered themselves atheists because they didn't agree with their parents' religiosity. As I looked at their Iron Maiden and Metallica T-shirts, I felt like I'd heard the same stories from young people in São Paulo.

Some of the examples I share might sound like I'm just talking about certain subcultures or fringe groups. I have found that the characteristics and mindset I will describe as the Global Youth Culture represent the predominant and mainstream culture of young people in every city around the world. Think about how connected we are today. The majority of the world population lives in urban centres linked together through high-speed online communication, social media, and a powerfully influential entertainment industry. This generation now shares a fast-moving and ever-changing global culture.

For the majority of history, culture originated and developed in the context of family and tradition. But the current information era with its ever advancing technology and communications have drastically changed the way our stories, art, and customs are shared. We used to learn about life by asking our parents and reading books. Now we turn to YouTubers like PewDiePie and Casey Neistat to tell us what to think about life, what to do with our time, what products to buy, and even how to vote.

To put it simply, the stories and values coming from social media and the entertainment industry are far more influential among young people today than those stories and values from their family and traditions, whether it be in Western countries, or anywhere else in the world with an Internet connection.

Already in 2011, an article in the *Guardian* described how "kids get their culture, gossip, and attitudes from Google and Facebook. They are constantly on, constantly promoting themselves and constantly connected". The article also quoted an academic study, by professor of social psychology Sonia Livingstone: "The web has become the place where young people most find their opportunity to explore and express their identities and their social relations, and navigate their way through the values that are on offer around them".[1]

By 2018, US statistics show 95 percent of youth have access to a smartphone and 45 percent say they are online almost constantly.[2]

Across the Atlantic the numbers are similar, where, in the Netherlands, "29 percent of 18 to 24-year-olds were addicted to social media in their own view"[3] and 83 percent of the adult population in the UK are now using one or more social media channels.[4]

A friend who recently visited China experienced a traditional meal sitting at a large round table that, in the past, represented an important part of family life—the opportunity to be together while sharing food and a story or two. Yet, as he looked around at the younger generation seated there, every one of them was engrossed in a different type of gathering on their smartphones, hearing and watching stories from the global network.

When my family moved to Brazil in 1992, we lived in an area surrounded by blocks of flats on quiet roads. My sisters and I played on the street most afternoons, where we learned the language and customs of our new home. We learned about *caipira* (Brazilian country music) parties and *Saci-pererê* (a Brazilian folk fairytale), marbles and kites, skateboards and football, yo-yos and Super Nintendos all in our neighbourhood, within a circle of friends and acquaintances. Although many products that became part of our environment were introduced from other countries via television commercials or big outdoor advertisements, the cultural trends were shared locally.

The first time I really perceived the power and speed of this new environment was when a local Curitiba band went viral overnight with a YouTube video in 2011. Of course, "going viral" was already around as early as 2007 when random homemade videos like "Charlie Bit My Finger" started to get views in the millions. But I hadn't experienced that so close to home, or realised how a local expression could suddenly go global. A Banda Mais Bonita da Cidade released a song called "Oração," and in less than a month it had reached over 6 million people. They were not the only band or artistic expression discovering this new way of sharing their material. The music and cultural scene in Brazil were changing fast, as were the cultural scenes in most large cities around the world.

Fast-forward a decade and you have artists like Billie Eilish, who, at sixteen, released her debut EP in August 2017 and reached 132 million streams on Spotify alone by October 2018. Her current, almost entirely sold-out world tour through Australia, Asia, Europe, and the US shows how globally connected we have become.

A shift in culture means changes in all areas of life. Dating has become a global activity, with apps like Tinder boasting 50 million users from 196 countries.[5] The mobilising power of our connectivity is also evident in charitable or social causes like the ALS Ice Bucket Challenge or #BlackLivesMatter. Even celebrities like former President Obama, Lady Gaga, and Bill Gates joined in the social media viral campaign that helped ALS Association raise more than $115 million for research toward Lou Gehrig's Disease. Black Lives Matter mobilised a whole social-political movement, with the hashtag #BlackLivesMatter being used over 12 million times on Twitter.[6]

Ironically, these technological advances that surpass geographical boundaries and would seem to better connect people with each other, are in some ways leading us further apart. Various studies over the past few years have shown that higher connectivity on social media can actual have the opposite affect, leading to an increased sense of loneliness. A study of university students in the UK found that their real life social interaction decreased with excessive use of Twitter, leading to a sense of loneliness.[7] And as one *Psychology Today* article puts it, "social media such as Facebook have become surrogates for seeking connectedness, and as a consequence our connections grow broader but shallower".[8]

Undeniably, social media is changing the way we relate to each other. One feature I heard Facebook was testing suggests topics for conversation with specific friends. Things like "Adam just visited the national gallery, ask him what he thought of it". These platforms have created a fast and impersonal way to constantly stay in touch with everyone I've ever known, yet with no depth or commitment.

Loneliness is not the only side effect of the fast-and-furious tendency of our global culture. British online newspaper the *Independent* recently released an article stating that using social media "too frequently can make you feel increasingly unhappy and isolated in the long run". It describes how comparing our lives with the carefully tailored profiles and photos of others leads users to struggle with low self-esteem, while compulsively looking at social media feeds can cut into our sleep and affect our attention span. It concludes that this online lifestyle can also lead to more serious mental health issues, quoting one particular survey in which 41 percent of participants claimed their social media usage makes them feel anxious and depressed.[9]

Another important change to realise in this global culture is the physical ease of mobility. We're not only connected online, but we are more prone to move around a world that seems much smaller than decades ago. Polish sociologist Zygmunt Bauman described a current "time-space compression," which happens not only because of the new speed at which information flies around the globe, but also the rapid development of methods of transportation.[10]

The World Tourism Organisation released research showing that 2016 was the seventh consecutive year of sustained growth in international tourism, with a total of 1235 million travellers worldwide.[11] The fastest growing age segment in international travel are young people sixteen to thirty-four, estimated by the United Nations to be 20 percent of all international tourists. And the way the younger generation travel is different too, being more based on a search for meaningful experiences, "exploring more remote destinations, staying in hostels instead of hotels, and choosing long-term backpacking trips instead of two-week jaunts".[12]

No wonder Zygmunt Bauman describes our global culture as "liquid". We are always on the move. We can't settle. We don't stay in one place, be it physically or digitally. Life has become increasingly fast paced. There's never enough time. No time to meet and build real relationships. No time to think about the big questions of life, about our purpose, and the meaning of it all.

Ease of movement, and the speed with which we continue to do it, eliminates our capacity to wait and to commit, leaving us restless, in a constant state of anxiety and dissatisfaction. We find it hard to concentrate, persist in the pursuit of a goal, keep a long-term relationship, maintain a job, or stay long enough in any thought or situation to truly commit to it.

This leaves us with no sense of purpose, replacing it with a drive to keep moving forward, finding the next hype, focusing on the here and now. We find ourselves in a vacuum with no end or conclusion in sight. As Bauman puts it "in this chase after new desires, rather than after their satisfaction, there is no obvious finishing line".[13]

This global culture brings huge changes in how we see ourselves, our communities, and the world. It changes our world from being a series of separate local communities to being one large and mobile mass. It has reshaped how we live our lives and even what we believe. Of course, there are still local cultural differences, but a key point to be understood here is that, for this internationally mobile and Internet-native generation, global trumps local. In this sense, it is reasonable to say that the Global Youth Culture is the largest united culture in history. And, in effect, the largest culture unreached by the gospel today.

We Are Consumers

In a 2008 MTV research study, young people in Brazil characterized themselves using three predominant words: *vanity*, *consumerism*, and *indifference*.[14] Consumerism is one of the main driving forces behind this global culture. Growing up bombarded by the entertainment industry, flooded by waves of new pleasure-seeking experiences, superficial solutions, and fast food, we have become addicted. Addicted to products, technology, Netflix, superficial relationships, sex, drugs and rock 'n' roll. We are the generation that wants more and wants it now, but we don't really know *what* we want.

We believe we can buy our identities through consumer choice: the clothes we wear, the music we listen to, the posts we share on social media, the products we consume. All this defines who we are. But the options are infinite, leaving us dazed and confused, unable to define ourselves. This leads to an identity crisis. Who are we and what are we living for? Is this all there is?

Bauman shows how closely consuming relates to identity in the consumer culture. "The way present-day society shapes its members is dictated first and foremost by the duty to play the role of the consumer".[15] This is so strongly the case that to resist these consumer desires and practises is an affront to the system. Maybe one of the most subversive attitudes to have in the consumer society is to be satisfied with what we have and who we are.

In a similar way, consumerism affects our relationships. We start to treat people like we treat stuff. With no time for commitment, we use a relationship while it benefits us, while it satisfies. As it grows old, we become impatient, wanting to step into the next new thing. We easily dispose of people who no longer serve our purposes, moving on from them with little or no consequence. And so relationships become fragile, temporary, and superficial. As Lucas Nord's song keeps repeating on my Spotify playlist, "I don't need your love no more, I don't need your love no more".

Holding self-sufficient independence and individuality so precious, we keep people at a safe distance. "Not togetherness, but avoidance and separation have become major survival strategies in the contemporary megalopolis".[16]

In identity crises and broken relationships, we easily turn to addiction. Pornography has become a normal part of our culture, defended by many psychologists and sexologists as a healthy stimulus for relationships. Current statistics state that 79 percent of young men view pornography at least once a month, and 76 percent of young women view it with the same frequency. Sixty percent of young men view porn several times a week.[17] But this sexuality packaged up for consumption fuels a multi-million-dollar industry and leads to addiction, cynicism, inability to commit to one partner, lack of trust, and broken families.

Maybe one of our biggest addictions is social media, with around 20 percent of users unable to go a few hours without checking Facebook, and 28 percent of iPhone users checking their Twitter feed before getting up in the morning.[18]

For the younger consumers in particular, video games become the addictive escape. A study of three thousand children and teenagers showed 72 percent of households had video games, and the average usage was twenty hours per week. That's the equivalent of a part-time job.[19]

Addiction kills our passion. This is the final effect of consumerism: indifference. We're numbed by the insatiable search for immediate pleasure. We read a book or watch a movie that inspires us, and we think we might do something with our lives, that maybe we could change the world. But then the next distracting source of entertainment comes along, or we go shopping, and that revolutionary thought slips away.

The year we had the amazing opportunity to take our show to the Middle East, we had concerts booked in Beirut and various cities in Turkey. But we had a logistical challenge, as we needed to get our equipment from Beirut to Istanbul. The best solution was to drive it. Back in 2007, before the Syrian conflict, this was a reasonably viable option. We just needed someone to drive the equipment van for us. I thought it would be easy to find a volunteer for that. I mean what an exciting summer volunteer opportunity, to tour across the Middle East with a rock band, sharing Jesus and making a real difference.

But no one responded to our mass email advertising the position. It was the year the game Call of Duty 4 came out, and I remember thinking of these dudes walking through the Middle East with a machine gun on a flat screen TV, thinking of themselves as heroes, yet with no passion to actually do something meaningful, like drive a van bringing peace to a broken region. Consumerism kills our passion. It turns us into zombies. Eventually, a father and son from New Zealand responded to the call and had the life-changing experience of serving the mission together in an unreached part of the world.

We're connected yet lonely. We can travel everywhere and have unending information at our fingertips, yet we're anxious and dissatisfied. Consumerism leads to identity crisis, superficial relationships, and addiction. Addiction leads to loss of passion. We are the generation that has grown up surrounded by this reality. Who can tell us who we are? Who can teach us what it means to love and be loved? How can we find a passion and purpose to live?

4

What You Believe Matters

"**L**ife is hard. You have to fight, and you have to believe in yourself. Don't listen to what others think. You are able. You can do something awesome with your life! That's our message. We're not standing under the flag of any religion or politics. Just have faith, believe in something!"

As I stood there listening to this São Paulo–based hardcore band and the thin tattooed figure of the lead singer passionately preaching his message, it felt convincing and generally positive but something just didn't seem to add up. If everything's okay and we just have to believe in ourselves, if we are truly able, then why aren't we getting anywhere. Why do we feel so alone when we put our heads on our pillows at night? Why do so many say they have no passion or purpose in life?

Too often I'd heard a very different perspective when it came to deeper conversations. When we toured round the world with No Longer Music, we often filmed street interviews. This really helped us understand how people thought, what their beliefs and questions were. One time we were interviewing people outside a venue in São Paulo asking, "What's your purpose in life? What are your dreams and ambitions?" One girl answered: "I don't know. I'm one of the many young people who don't have dreams anymore".

Most of the time we just get on with life and don't think too much about these issues. Once we did this same set of interviews in Wellington, New Zealand. One girl answered: "Just have fun, enjoy yourself. If you spend your whole life looking for a point, you're going to miss it . . . because there is no point".

I've wanted to respond by sharing how I've found hope and purpose in Jesus. But I discovered early on that the global culture follows a very different set of values and view of life. On one occasion, in conversation with a group of young people in front of a club, we got to the topic of belief in God. One guy explained "I believe there may be a god, or whatever you want to call it, but he doesn't interfere with our lives".

The first time I encountered this was in university. It, like most art colleges, held strongly to humanistic and secular values, encouraging liberalism and tolerance with everything – but religion. My faith was dismissed as my own opinion, and mostly irrelevant to them.

Despite being told my faith shouldn't come into my work and studies, I found it almost impossible to avoid, as it is so central to who I am. In my final dissertation, I decided to write about how much our worldview affects everything we do. I went round asking students and teachers some of those big questions that identify a worldview, like What is the meaning of life? or How do you define beauty and goodness? Interestingly one of the most common answers was I don't know. I'd never thought much about that.

But what you believe does matter. If I believe I can fly, then jumping off the roof of my house shouldn't matter – until I break a leg. If I believe I can handle driving while drunk, then I'll get behind the wheel – until I kill a person and get sentenced to prison. If I believe that unborn babies aren't persons and support killing them, eventually human life won't mean much to me anymore.

Most of my colleagues were living by the predominant secular humanist mindset of our time, often without ever having thought much about it. Whether it be watching trends on social media, meeting people on the streets and in clubs, or going to university, you get the sense that that mindset has become global. On the surface, it seems people have hope and a desire to see change. That they believe change is possible and that people are capable of doing good. But when I dug deeper and asked bigger life questions, I found hopelessness, despair, a lack of purpose and confusion.

Where does this mindset come from? Where do we get our common values in this global culture?

Today's Global Worldview

The global culture described in the last chapter is not only connecting us or trying to sell us something. It is creating a unified worldview that gradually takes over any local, traditional or religious worldview.

A worldview is man's reflection and conclusions about life and the world around him. From the professor of philosophy to the illiterate, consciously or unconsciously, everyone has a worldview.[1] But this, of course, is not something we pull out of thin air. Our worldview very much relates to and comes from our context and the main influencing voices around us. We are always influenced by the zeitgeist, the spirit of the time. And in the context of globalisation, a global zeitgeist, powerfully driven by the fastest and most efficient communication medium man has ever seen, will certainly be the primary driving influence on an individual's personal worldview.

Today's global culture holds one predominant worldview: secular humanism. It is taught in our schools and universities, used by economic strategies, advertisement, and the entertainment industry. It is emphasised in the consumer lifestyle sold on television and the Internet and preached by the majority of this generation on social media.

Humanism itself is simply affirming the inherent value of human beings. It is a positive view of the potential and beauty of humankind, something that most religions, Christianity included, would agree with. But the predominant form of humanism we see propagated today is secular humanism, which takes a step further, saying human beings not only have value and potential but that we are central and self-sufficient.

The 1973 Humanist Manifesto declares: "No deity will save us; we must save ourselves," and "We are responsible for what we are and for what we will be".[2] This thinking makes mankind the reference of truth, morality, and purpose and the central piece to the progression of society. It is a worldview that rejects formal moral systems and plunges society into an amorality that idolises independence and individual choice.

Secular humanism is, therefore, the perfect partner for the consumer drive of this global culture. This "survival of the fittest" perspective and materialistic focus needs a worldview with no clear morality or purpose, only a desire for profit. In fact, it is quite hard to say whether it was the secular humanist worldview that led to consumer culture or whether consumer culture paved the way for this worldview. Either way, consumerism encourages and is encouraged by secular humanism.

Because it has become the predominant majority worldview, secular humanism is now the norm. It's just how things are; it's what everyone thinks, and therefore, it is accepted without question. Secular humanism pretends to be tolerant while bullying any other worldview or faith to the margins.

So what exactly are we all being told to believe? What is secular humanism anyway?

Desperate

Secular Humanism says there is no truth. Truth cannot be defined. Francis Schaeffer, one of the great Christian minds of the twentieth century, described this shift in the way we see truth as "stepping below the line of despair".[3]

It started with revolt. A reaction to long-standing Christian view and values that led to our current post-Christian society. The Enlightenment, the eighteenth-century Age of Reason, questioned everything, including Christianity and religion in general. Initially, the Enlightenment movement assumed there was truth out there but increasingly distanced itself from biblical authority. Instead, humanity turned to science and philosophy.

While rejecting the Christian meta-narrative, philosophers continued to attempt to close all ideas and concepts into one all-encompassing truth. But this rationalist mission of Enlightenment also failed. We couldn't find an all-encompassing truth in philosophy, and we gradually lost confidence in science being able to find all the answers. This led to a second revolt, this time against modernist rationality itself. This rejection of the modernist dream of finding and defining truth became known as Postmodernism.

The well-known American evangelical theologian and philosopher Francis Schaeffer describes this moment: "Above the line of despair men were rationalistic optimists. . . . It was as though the rationalists suddenly became trapped in a large round room with no doors and no windows, nothing but complete darkness".[4]

When we question everything unendingly, pulling everything apart, deconstructing every institution and concept, we end up with nothing but darkness. As C. S. Lewis once pointed out: "You can't go on 'seeing through' things forever. The whole point of seeing through something is to see something through it. To 'see through' all things is the same as not to see".[5]

This was Schaeffer's "stepping below the line of despair," concluding that truth can no longer be defined by anyone, be it religion, science, or philosophy. The reference for truth was no longer Christianity or science, but ourselves, our own opinions. Truth became relative; it now depends on each person's point of view.

Schaeffer explains that this happens in stages, like a staircase, through the following spheres of culture consecutively: philosophy, art, music, general culture and then even theology. Captured by artists, who Schaeffer called "the sensitive souls," of our generation and passed on through their art and music, these same concepts reach the masses, the general culture. Once pop icons such as John Lennon were singing about it, the influence became global: "I believe in god, but not as one thing, not as an old man in the sky. I believe that what people call god is something in all of us".[6]

On the surface this worldview is confident and arrogant, putting mankind at the centre. It looks pretty, presenting seemingly positive values and an optimistic perspective. But deep down, denying any form of defined and absolute truth is like losing the floor beneath your feet. It creates a vacuum, a shallow temporal view of life. What matters is here and now. The only thing of importance is what I think and what I want. It has helped form a narcissistic, consumerist, and empty culture. Eventually, it leads us to a deep sense of lostness and hopeless despair.

Arrogant

In 2014 the British Humanist Society released a series of videos promoting the humanist worldview. They were narrated by one of my favourite British comedians, Stephen Fry. In the video entitled "What Makes Something Right or Wrong?" Fry explains: "Humanists do not look to any gods for rules but think carefully for themselves about what might be the best way to live".[7]

When you remove all reference to truth, reality, morality, or purpose it ultimately leaves each of us to figure things out for ourselves. Secular humanism puts us at the centre. We decide what we do with our lives. Individual choice is our ultimate value.

This was often the response I got when sharing my faith in university: "that's your opinion". A friend and I were in a deep conversation once when she brought up the story of the elephant and the blind men. A group of blind men feel the elephant and attempt to define what the elephant is like. One finds a leg and says the elephant is like a pillar; another finds the tail and says the elephant is like a rope; another the trunk and says it is like a tree branch; another feels an ear and says the elephant is like a fan; another finds the belly and describes the elephant as a wall; while another feels a tusk and describes it as a solid pipe. The narrator concludes that all of them are right. They just discovered the elephant from different perspectives.

On the surface, the argument seems to make sense, but as Timothy Keller points out in his book *The Reason for God*, it conceals a considerable arrogance in making everyone blind but the narrator himself. The narrator gets to decide on the final conclusion – the truth of the matter. Christianity and any other view are now considered one of the blind men, while the secular humanist stands as the current narrator telling the others they are all only partially right. "How could you possibly know that no religion can see the whole truth unless you yourself have the superior, comprehensive knowledge of spiritual reality you just claimed that none of the religions have?"[8]

It's crucial that we understand this. In the eyes of this predominant worldview, Christianity, the Bible, the Christian God are no more than one option among many others. And my consumeristic free choice takes priority over sacred texts and millennia of tradition, granting me the wisdom to say "this is true" and "that is not". Remember, truth can no longer be defined. Christianity, and religion in general, have become marginalised. According to the "tolerant" secular humanists, Christianity is still allowed a say in things but certainly not a front row seat, and it is generally received with scepticism and prejudice. This secularism has relegated religion to the margins of society.

But this arrogance is flawed. Secular humanism needs a dose of its own medicine. The rules it so faithful applies to all, it cannot and does not apply to itself. In saying there is no absolute truth, I am in fact defining an absolute truth. The fact is, relativism, as one of the basic premises of secular humanism, is deeply flawed and easily debunked. Its very core rationale shoots itself in the foot. It saws off the very branch it sits on. As it sets out questioning and deconstructing, it deconstructs itself. It is surprisingly fragile and superficial and yet preached as an unquestionable value, believed and accepted beyond doubt by those holding this globalised mindset.

Pretty . . . Pretty Vacant

So if there is no absolute truth, and we are the ones to define truth, right and wrong, and what we want to do with our own lives, then what is the meaning and purpose of life? How do we define that?

Terry Eagleton, a current humanist philosopher sought to answer this in his book *The Meaning of Life*: "A meaning to life put there by God, and one conjured up by ourselves, may not be the only possibilities. . . . Meaning is also an endlessly unfinished process, a shuffling from one sign to another without fear or hope of closure".[9]

In a way, the predominant humanist mindset is saying stop taking life so seriously, just chill and enjoy it! That's how we arrived at not really caring about a big meaning or purpose to life, or not worrying about what we believe in.

Eagleton concludes in his book that the meaning of life is to find happiness and love. It's so nice. On the surface, this seems a very positive, pretty, and acceptable way to see life. Just be happy and love one another. The problem is, have we not always been trying this? What man or woman in all history has not wanted to be happy or to love and be loved? And yet we seem no closer to it.

The real problem here is that when we destroy truth and morality and make ourselves the reference point, then who defines what is love and what is happiness? The whole mindset leaves us with so many unanswered questions, and as Eagleton pointed out, for a humanist, that's okay. We don't need to know. But I can't help thinking the whole thing is a big charade, a farce. If I can't define truth, then I can't define love and happiness, and yet this is what we're all searching for. This is what we're expected to live for. Empty words, with no real meaning behind them.

Social media is full of this charade. We say things that no longer have meaning but sound nice. Terrorists bomb Paris, and suddenly everyone Tweets out #PrayforParis or adds a photo filter to their Facebook profile. Our global culture teaches that no one can really define who we're praying to, or what praying really is, but it sounds nice to say I'm praying. We post and tweet pretty slogans about being happy and loving one another, we preach freedom and democracy, we believe we're progressing, heading somewhere good, we just don't know where that is.

We're told to believe in something, to have faith in faith. We've been taught to put on a brave face and say, "I'm fine". "I'm happy". This is what we call a leap of faith. When we have no reference point and our lives are void of meaning – "just be happy, enjoy life!" What on the surface seems great and acceptable is empty below. As a wise punk philosopher once said, "we're pretty . . . pretty vacant".

5

Lost

"Never have people thought so hard about their lives and come to such indecision, or felt further apart. We're powerless and confused – by politics and work and sex and even things like morality".[1]

This global consumer culture satisfies my immediate and more superficial desires. It gives me a false sense of identity and numbs the pain, but it doesn't speak to my heart. It doesn't touch my soul. It doesn't answer the big questions of life. If I want to know where the nearest restaurant is, I can turn to my smartphone. If I want to know who Friedrich Nietzsche was, I can look him up on Google. But if I'm looking for the meaning of life, or for hope, my smartphone can't help me.

And then the worldview on offer today, secular humanism, is supposed to answer these questions, but it tells me that no one can define anything beyond the material world. No one really knows the answers to the big questions, or at least not a final answer. We're being told we should simply look to ourselves. To come up with our own opinions. We are left alone with our thoughts, doubts, and despair. Or we can look to the millions of opinions of others on social media, which tends to make us more confused. We're told to just enjoy life, but it doesn't seem to work.

The Fear

Deep down we know there's something wrong. We put on that brave face; we say we're progressing and that all we need is love. But the art and pop scene can't help but cry out. Something's wrong; something is lacking.

Lily Allen sings it clearer than ever in her song "The Fear," saying she doesn't know how she's meant to feel. As she poetically describes the shallow narcissism of this global culture, Lily hits a surprising conclusion in the chorus. In this relativistic mindset she doesn't know what's right or real anymore, and yet there's a lingering fear hanging over her. Fear of what?

The fact is, even with this positive "feel good" humanistic worldview, we can't shake off the burden we carry. Deep down we know there's something wrong. We carry the weight of things we wish we hadn't done, of hurt caused by others toward us, and hurt we know we've caused others. We look at the world and know deep down we're not progressing. We see the wars, famine, and destruction caused by our own selfishness, and we don't know what to do with it. Maybe if we pretend it's not there, it will go away.

In the 2004 film *Eternal Sunshine of a Spotless Mind* a doctor develops a way to erase a selected part of a patient's memory. He makes money erasing mistakes clients wish they'd never made and romantic relationships they wish they'd never had. The problem was the patients, not remembering the mistakes they committed, simply committed the same mistakes again and again, in a cycle of self-destruction. We can't just forget our mistakes and pretend they never happened. Whether it be Hollywood or Spotify, the cry goes out concerning the deep awareness that something is wrong.

The Hunger

As the Florence and the Machine hit song goes, "we all have a hunger" – that empty feeling inside us, that loneliness, that weight with which our heads hit the pillow at night when we are all alone. It's part of being human, as if we're born with something missing, something beyond us and beyond this world.

British indie rock artist, Florence Welch, talked about this in a TV interview about her 2018 album *High as Hope*. She described her awareness of a needy love she had been trying to fill. "Something outside of me needs to fix this. . . . It's like, I can date the solution or I can drink the solution or take the solution. . . . This record is a recognition of 'Oh, you can't'!"[2]

When asked about her hit song "Hunger" Florence explained, "I was thinking about something bigger than romantic love. . . . The song kinda came from that idea like what is it I was looking for that was outside myself?"[3]

What, indeed. This, I believe is the key question we should all be asking. The current predominant mindset tells us there is nothing beyond what we see around us. We've been brought up to believe that all we need can be found within ourselves. But if we're honest, we know Florence is right. We need something bigger.

I was struck by an advert I saw a few years ago. It starts with a camera close up of a guy dramatically describing something that sounds like the most amazing thing in the world, maybe a revolution, the cure to cancer, or even God himself. But as the passionate narrative goes on, we start to see images of a car, until finally he announces: the all-powerful, awesome, praiseworthy thing is the new i8 BMW.

As a good friend of mine, professor Jonas Madureira, says "we have made the absolute relative and the relative absolute". Things that are supposed to be small details of our lives become the centrepiece, and that which is most important is forgotten. When we make ourselves the reference, we realise we are not sufficient, so we look for meaning elsewhere. As we now believe meaning cannot be defined, we are on a never-ending search for something we just can't find.

The sense that something is missing has led this generation to be spiritually open, seeking but never finding answers. Mistrust of institutions means that mainstream religion is generally pushed aside, but any other form of spirituality is often viewed with curiosity.

A friend at university once tried explaining her beliefs to me. "I'm Catholic, but I also believe in Umbanda (African-Brazilian black magic), and there are also aspects of witchcraft and Buddhism that I like. I try to meditate regularly to seek peace, but I don't think anyone can really define God".

After lessons, I often liked to walk across the street from my university campus and read the Bible in the park. Once a girl walked over and started up a conversation. "That's so cool you're reading the Bible. I love reading stuff like that. I read lots of spiritual literature and then I look inside myself to seek truth". I listened to her and then explained, "I would be so lost and confused if all I could do was look inside myself to find truth. I change my mind and get confused with my thoughts and feelings all the time".

The fact is that most of this global generation are interested in spirituality but not formal institutional religion. The shift in culture towards individualism and personal choice has changed how we view God and religion. We define our own belief system and can mix beliefs and ideas to fit our preferences. Religion falls among the many options and categories in our consumer habits. And at the end of the day, we are left with the unsettling sense that no one really knows what to believe in anymore.

The Dissatisfaction

We still hope we can change the world. Humanism has a positive perspective; it teaches we are progressing and that if we keep fighting, we will have a better world. So social and environmental causes are in fashion; people are going to the streets to protest. We want to fight but often we don't know what we're fighting for.

In 2011 hundreds of young people took to the streets across the UK in violent riots: "Away from the towers that soar above the City of London, there is another England. It is an ugly place. In this England, a million young people have their hopes blasted every day. In this England, thousands of work-starved youngsters search for jobs that do not exist. In this England, legions of kids find themselves crowded into sink estates that tower over streets absent of power and absent of hope. They are the England left behind by globalisation. And they are the England who, in 2011, took to the streets and smashed up their neighbourhoods".[4]

Kids were angry, but rather than a clear and coherent voice for change, we saw violence and chaos. Sociologists and journalists aren't sure why it happened and therefore don't know what can be done to keep it from happening again.

In 2013 Brazil saw the largest popular uprising on the streets in twenty years. Almost 2 million people participated in demonstrations in eighty cities across the country with approval from 84 percent of the general population.[5] According to official reports the initial cause was a rise in the cost of local bus tickets, but soon there was a huge mix of political groups and causes stamped on banners as millions took to the streets. Many people were asking at the time, what are we actually protesting? The common feeling seemed to be that everyone was angry about something and wanting some kind of change, but they couldn't quite explain what.

Probably the largest movement of protests we've seen in our global generation was the Arab uprising, which led to drastic political changes in the Arab world. It ended in overwhelming tragedy and violence, however. The worst consequence of the Arab Spring is the ongoing situation in war-torn Syria. This was very much an expression of the global youth of the Arab world.

I remember meeting young people from Syria in Beirut when the war was just starting. They were creative, connected, and full of hope. They were fully aware, and involved in the global conversation, and dreamed of change. And it was the tools of the global culture that they used to spread their message.

Journalist Paul Danahar described Saudi Arabia as experiencing "widespread resentment and frustration from large sections of its young population who want to see change. They talk about it incessantly online, which is the only public forum they have. By 2013 more of its population were using Twitter than in any other country in the world".[6]

Yet, no matter where these protests happen, one thing seems to remain. We want change; we just don't know what that change looks like or how to make it happen. When we don't know what is right and true, we can't change the world.

People at my university were often talking about different causes and wanting to be part of a movement to bring change. One time there was a demonstration called the "March for Freedom". When I first heard of the protest I thought, "great, I believe in freedom. It will be cool to be part of that". But when the day of the protest came, it was clear the majority were marching for legalising cannabis and abortion. I realised the freedom they marched for was not what I call freedom. In fact, it seemed tragic that freedom for these young university students was freedom to smoke dope and abort unwanted babies.

We want change, but we don't know what we want.

The Emptiness

The toxic combination of a secular humanist worldview in a consumer driven culture is making us shallow narcissists, fixating on our image. We are obsessed with selfies and health fads and numbing our minds with crude and shallow entertainment on YouTube. The trends on

Twitter and Facebook seem to feed off that humanist idol: my own personal opinion. Everybody has an opinion about everything, and it must be heard.

Sharing personal opinion has even spawned a new form of star, the YouTuber. Some of the most influential people on the planet, having their voice heard by the largest audiences, are basically just sharing their opinions about very normal day-to-day topics, with homemade videos. I mentioned YouTuber PewDiePie in chapter 3. In 2018 he became the first ever to hit 70 million subscribers on his channel. The Swede, Felix Kjellberg, started in 2011 posting video game commentary videos and later expanded to comedy and vlogs. It's the simple day-to-day nature of the content that seems to draw the masses. It's the wave of reality shows, now morphed into independent productions made by anyone with a connected smartphone.

If we're listening, we can hear that cry again. The cry of a lost generation, seeking truth in themselves – and finding emptiness. I don't know what's true anymore or who I am, but maybe if I voice my opinions and show myself to the world, other people can tell me who I am and what is true. The trouble is we're often not really listening. Watching a YouTuber can be nothing more than a desperate look in the mirror, identifying with that same sense of angst as we ask ourselves "what is this all about after all and who cares?"

The mass influence of this mindset and culture has reached alarming proportions, trickling into every area of life, influencing even the very top of the international political scene. The shallowness and amorality of the global culture are now characteristic of some of the most influential political leaders on the global stage. The state we have reached is one where unverified Facebook posts upstage well-researched news reporting, and on Twitter it seems to be "survival of the vilest" defines public opinion and wins elections.

Sadly, the sense of emptiness often leads to more serious issues. Reports of mental health crises among young people have now become common place, some calling it a "silent catastrophe". One survey of teachers labelled it an "epidemic" in the UK.[7]

Without a doubt, we're facing a crisis of purpose, and suicide has become an increasingly more prevalent theme in pop culture. Whether it be Netflix series like *13 Reasons Why*, nihilist meme trends on social media, or the growing number of hit songs addressing it, there's no doubt this is an issue on our minds.

Tragically, suicide is not just a trending topic but a stark reality. Art and music are simply voicing the facts we see in a lost generation, facing a lack of meaning. The World Hope Organisation reports that suicide is currently the second leading cause of death among young people aged fifteen to twenty-nine.[8] The problem is often highlighted in the music scene as seemingly an increasing number of rock and pop icons commit suicide. In 2018 young and rising trap artist Lil Peep lost his life to overdose and two major rock names – Chris Cornell and Chester Bennington – took their own lives.

Clearly, people are searching for answers, and as Jesus' followers, we need to know how to respond. How can we bring hope in such a void? Writing and singing about it is important, but a lot of the answers offered in the current scene don't sit right with me.

Rapper Logic raises awareness of depression and suicide in his song "1-800-273-8255". It follows the story of a young guy coming out gay and then contemplating ending his life. As the title (the number for the US National Suicide Prevention Lifeline) suggests, the answer given is to seek help when you're down. This is, of course, sound advice, but it doesn't really confront the true issue of hopelessness. It's no surprise that a generation growing up without any clear reference for questions surrounding morality, sexuality, and purpose, experiences confusion and despair. People need to know the truth about their souls, otherwise no helpline will do.

The duo Twenty One Pilots (TOP) often addresses deep issues through creative and poetic lyrics, and a couple of their songs talk about suicide. "Please Friend" seems to depict a conversation between friends, in which one seeks to convince the other not to take his own life.

The song that stood out to me, however, was "Kitchen Sink". This song doesn't specifically address suicide, but reflects on the question of purpose, or the lack of it. A friend recently shared a post about "Kitchen Sink" that read, "I feel like this song pretty well encapsulates that push and pull of who to trust, a search for identity, an exasperated rejection of those around, undercut by the four words, 'Don't leave me alone'".

In an interview last year, Tyler (lead singer of TOP), revealed some of his thoughts behind these lyrics. While his good intentions were clear – wanting to reach out to people facing depression and suicidal thoughts – his advice circling around self-help felt empty. Trying to derive strength and a sense of purpose from our own creativity and uniqueness just isn't enough. We all know that. If we have nothing but ourselves to trust, then we will be constantly frustrated. This is why a culture fixated on selfies and self-promotion fails to find sense and purpose. We were made for more than this.

We need to be part of this conversation. The apostle Peter wrote, "Always be prepared to give an answer to everyone who asks you to give the reason for the hope that you have. But do this with gentleness and respect" (1 Peter 3:15). My prayer is that we might bring a message of hope, not based on our own abilities and "inner self" but on the hope we have in Jesus. If we stand on that solid Rock, we can know what is right and wrong, what brings life and what destroys it, what is true and false, and ultimately what we were made for.

The cry of the Global Youth Culture rings out loud and clear. This generation is lost, and thirsty for truth. Who will go to them?

6

The Source of Hope

I learned a lot in my years at university in Curitiba while simultaneously touring with No Longer Music. But it was the deep awareness of the spiritual need of this globalised generation that marked me more than any of my studies or international travel.

I'll never forget a show we did in Odemira, Portugal, where a group of young guys had started their own cultural association and put together a festival for local bands. They were mostly into the skater scene and hardcore music. At the end of our concert, I told the crowd of around three hundred people that Jesus was there and wanted a personal relationship with them. I invited people to come and kneel in front of the stage with me if they wanted to know Jesus. Around thirty people came and knelt with me, including some of the young organisers.

One came up to me afterwards and told me that he had heard this message before. He explained that there was a missionary in Odemira who had started a Bible study with young people from the local skater scene, but later he left because his church didn't agree with what he was doing. I guess a Bible study for these secular skater kids wasn't what the church wanted their missionary to be involved in, so they called him home. Now here's this young guy telling me he wanted to know more about Jesus but didn't know where to go. My heart broke for him and his friends.

It made me think of the spiritual desert in which so many of my generation live. No matter where we are, whenever we have boldly shared the message of Jesus in a relevant and clear way, we have encountered a deep thirst for truth. When people get the chance to meet Jesus and understand who He truly is, they are drawn to Him. Yet so few get the chance to hear about Jesus in this way. Around 54 percent of the world population currently lives in urban centres. That's nearly 4 billion people. The 2 billion young people in this urban setting, part of the Global Youth Culture I've described, have very little chance of hearing who Jesus is in a way that makes sense to them.[1] Two billion people.

Europe, often referred to as the secular continent, is in dire need of churches and people willing to engage the global culture and boldly share the gospel. Less than 2 percent claim to know Jesus personally, and vast numbers of towns and cities have no church to teach them about having a personal relationship with Jesus.[2] And those that do, the churches are not communicating the gospel in a relevant way.

How can this global generation find the truth? How can the skater kids in Odemira have the opportunity to meet the living Jesus? And how can young people with no church background find a place to encounter the transformational Word of God and grow in their faith? I've described an unreached generation moving full speed ahead and driven by consumerism. One that's influenced by a global worldview that teaches us to vainly focus on ourselves and our own personal choice yet is desperately lost, afraid, confused, and dissatisfied. Faced with these challenges, how can we share Jesus and make disciples in the Global Youth Culture?

I was convinced God had called me to reach this culture, and yet I felt inadequate before this huge challenge. I knew it would not come through good strategies and human ideas. To reach the Global Youth Culture and challenge such a predominant and opposing mindset in our society today, we desperately need God's power. To share hope with people, we first need to know Him, the source of hope. I had already seen the power of prayer on the streets of Curitiba and on tour with NLM, and I knew more than ever that I needed God if I was to do anything significant in response to this reality.

Seek God

When I surrender to this awesome and all-powerful God, I not only find hope, but I gain the amazing privilege of being called his friend and walking with Him day by day. He is the source of hope, identity, vision, inspiration, and power. How precious it is to stand before the almighty God, Creator of the universe, who invites us to be part of His plan and mission!

I have very few memories from when I was six years old, but one clearly stands out in my mind till this day. I was sitting on my bed with my mother, and she was reading the story of Jesus receiving children: "Let the little children come to me, and do not hinder them, for the kingdom of heaven belongs to such as these" (Matt. 19:14). My mother asked me if I wanted to be one of these children of the kingdom of God. I realised then that He wanted me and was inviting me to come to Him. I said yes. Before calling us to do something for Him, Jesus calls us to be with Him and to be His.

Every key moment of realising who I was and my purpose in this world came from spending time with God. When I was twelve years old and decided I wanted to be baptised, I walked in my backyard and prayed, "God what do you want to do in my life? Tell me, and I will do it". At the baptism the minister said, "I don't usually have this sort of clear prophetic word from God, but I believe He is calling you to be a man of the Word and that you will share the Word in different places round the world in a unique way that He will show you in the right time". God answers prayers, and as we spend time with Him, He shows us who we are and His heart for us.

When I was in university and had a job teaching English in Brazil, my boss had this little shack out in the hills near Curitiba. The shack was a three-hour walk from the nearest town and had no running water or electricity. He never used it, as he only had it hoping to renovate it one day, so I asked him if I could go spend a weekend there.

"What are you going to do there?" he asked, looking at me like I was mad.

"I'm going to pray," I explained.

"What like a monk or something?" he asked, even more concerned about my sanity.

"Well, I guess so, yes".

The first night there, I lay my head on the pillow and was convinced I could hear something like a tribal drumbeat in the distance. I started wondering if there was an indigenous tribe somewhere in the area but then realised I was hearing the sound of my own heartbeat. I'd never been in such absolute silence and solitude. It was the first time I really noticed the sound of my own breathing and heartbeat.

I took nothing but a Bible and some water and spent the days walking around the countryside crying out to God. One day I decided I would walk to the top of the highest hill and watch the sunset. By the time the sun had gone down, I realised it was too dark to find my way back to the shack. I lay down to try to sleep up there in the warm summer night. After a while I started hearing the noises of nature all around me and freaked out. I realised there was some kind of burrow near me and was convinced I could hear something moving around inside. I jumped up and started blindly striding through the long grass and bushes trying to find a way down the hill. After a long frantic walk, I somehow found my way back to the protection of the little shack. Praying has often got me lost, but I guess it just means more praying in the end.

On the wall at the Steiger International Training Centre in Germany is the phrase "God rewards those who seek Him with a desperate heart". This is our number one value. During our mission school every Friday is Seek God Day. We start the day with silent prayer in the main hall, where we gather and pray for each other, blessing one another as we go out on a day with Jesus. Then we all go off, adhering to a vow of silence for the day (no talking to each other). Some go for long walks, some sit in a park, others go to the quiet of their rooms, but all pray, read the Bible, and listen to God.

For most people the first time they spend eight hours in prayer is daunting. "What will I pray about for eight hours?" they think. But by the end of the 10-week course, most students will say it was the most important part of the school. When we stop long enough and bring everything before Him in prayer and listen to his voice by reading the word, it's amazing what clear direction and vision we can receive from God.

Seek God with Your wife (or husband if you're a girl)

I attended the Steiger Mission School straight after university, which at the time was in New Zealand. Not bad! What an incredible place. But what I loved most about the school was the emphasis on spending time with God. It's always been like that and still is. I'd spend hours walking on those beautiful beaches asking God what was on His heart, and what He wanted me to do.

One time walking along the beach I met a guy walking his dog. I had already been impressed with the friendliness of Kiwis (the people, not the bird), but nothing prepared me for this.

"Hello!" I said as I walked by.

"Aw, you alright mate?" responded friendly-dog-walker. "Where you from then, aye?" he inquired. That was always a hard question to answer for me. But we got talking. Out of the blue he asked "Have you been around other parts of New Zealand to see the sights?"

"No not yet," I explained, "but me and some friends were thinking of going on a trip next week".

"Do you want to take my van?" he asked.

"What?" I said, pretty sure I'd misunderstood. "But you just met me!" I exclaimed.

"Nah, it's cool. Go for it. You can pick it up tomorrow". He said, as if he was lending me a lawnmower.

"Well how much do you want for it?" I asked, expecting there to be a catch.

"Pack o' cigarettes," he answered.

So the next week we went all around the North Island with a bunch from the school, in friendly-dog-walker's van.

That trip turned out to be pretty important. That's when it became clear to me that Ania was the girl I was supposed to marry. We'd met the year before, when I was on tour with NLM. She organised one of our concerts in Poland, where she's from. She didn't really notice me at first, but I certainly noticed her. I had just crossed the border from Germany to Poland in a VW van with the band. I was sitting next to David, who you will remember is the founder of Steiger and No Longer Music. He turns to me and says "Luke, in Poland there are many beautiful and crazy girls. You should choose one and marry her". So I did.

After dating for a month and a half, I proposed to this fiery, godly woman, who had the same passion as I did to see God's mission fulfilled. We sat at the top of a mountain in Kapiti coast and committed ourselves to Jesus. We didn't want to waste any time. We were determined to team up and begin the exciting task of sharing Jesus with this generation.

We decided the best time to get married was that summer, during the NLM tour, when all our friends would be around. I asked David to go on a walk with me. "David I'd like to marry Ania". "That's a great idea!" he said. I continued, "we thought the best time would be in the middle of the NLM tour". He just looked at me. I waited for him to tell me this wasn't sensible. Instead he said, "Rock on!"

We got married in Poland, after touring Germany with No Longer Music. Our first two weeks of marriage were spent sharing Jesus in Turkey. And we loved it. I played drums and she filmed everything, making short documentary films about what God was doing through the tour.

After that we moved to the UK. For some years I had wanted to attend a place called All Nations in Hertfordshire, England. It's a mission training centre in a beautiful mansion in the countryside, where the Buxton family used to organise prayer meetings for missionaries like Hudson Taylor, who had been a family friend.

First, we went to spend time with my home church in Southwest London. It was during this time that we ran that cafe for the local youth I mentioned in chapter 1. We didn't have anywhere to live, so a kind elderly lady from the church let us stay in her spare room. Some couples wait until they have everything to get married. That never made sense to me, as I think you miss out on the adventure of figuring life out together! Also, it's often at life's pivotal moments – getting married, starting a career, having a family – that we can lose sight of God's calling on our lives. God had always provided for me, and I knew that now he would provide for my family too. So we weren't going to wait around and let life pass by. We wanted to give everything we had for the things we knew mattered the most.

We needed to save some money to be able to attend the training at All Nations, and if you want money you have to work. So Ania got a job cleaning houses and looking after people with special needs, and I got a job as a painter-decorator assistant.

One of the first things Ania said to me after we were married was that we had to learn to seek God together. I didn't know what she meant. I mean, I knew how to pray, but she was going on about finding our way of connecting with God together. It all sounded a bit mystical to me. But she really challenged me to pray more, and to do it as a couple.

In 1 Samuel 25 there is an amazing story of courage and conviction. A rich Calebite man named Nabal was married to a beautiful and intelligent woman named Abigail. Nabal was a surly man who rejected David's request for food and supplies even though David's men were kind to Nabal's shepherds. Abigail intervenes at risk of her own life and stops David from storming off to kill Nabal, a man who had wronged him. David is impressed and blesses her for stopping him from making a mistake and pointing him back to God. I think that's exactly what we should look for in a wife (or a husband) – an Abigail spirit. I'm so thankful for a wife who points me to God when I'm losing track.

Once we had enough money to rent our own flat, we moved into a little one-bedroom place nearby in Sutton. It belonged to one of the church elders. His mother had lived there previously, so the place looked like it was straight out of the seventies.

We didn't mind; we were happy to have our first place. As most couples do, we started thinking about how we wanted to make it like home. One of the first things we both thought of was a prayer room. So we covered the living room in white sheets, some cushions, a little coffee table and candles everywhere. For some reason we thought that would create a good prayer atmosphere. It didn't occur to us to run a good old "health and safety" risk assessment as you do in England, so we hadn't really thought about the potential fire hazard. But apparently this was all very dangerous, as we soon found out when the church elder who owned the place came to visit. He pointed out the dangers of our prayer room and told us to take all the sheets and candles down.

But that didn't stop us from having awesome prayer times together. I bought a guitar so we could sing worship songs and spend time seeking God. We asked him to show us what He wanted us to do. That was how we had the idea for the cafe for young people. Any significant idea we had came from our prayer times with God. We came to realise time before God is precious. It gives you His perspective, reminds you what really matters, puts you in tune with his Spirit, and fills you with faith and boldness to do what he calls you to do.

Seek God for Vision and Power

Every time I've seen God move powerfully, it started with a vision born in prayer. When we started the cafe for young people in the London area, it began with a small group of us crying out to God for the young people in our neighbourhood. Steiger and No Longer Music started from David and Jodi and their team in Amsterdam spending nights out in the forest crying out to God. Each of the initiatives I share in the next few chapters was born out of time seeking God, asking him for His heart for the lost and His vision to effectively reach this generation.

When David Wilkerson decided to stop watching TV every night and spend time in prayer instead, God gave him a vision to reach marginalised young people in New York City. During a prayer time, this country preacher was drawn to a magazine article describing a murder case against a group of delinquent teens. Wilkerson was deeply moved by God, and his life was drastically changed. That same week he drove to New York and started a ministry to reach gangs and outcasts that became Teen Challenge, an inspirational mission helping the marginalised and those in addiction all over the world. You can trace the life of any seriously impactful man or woman of God back to a habit of prayer. Martin Luther supposedly once said, "I have so much to do that I shall spend the first three hours in prayer".

During the time in that little flat in Sutton I was reading *The Heavenly Man* a story of Brother Yun. Living in the interior of China, Yun had no access to a Bible, but his mother had met Jesus, and Yun's father had been miraculously healed from cancer after the family prayed to Jesus for healing. So Brother Yun wanted to know more. Yun was only sixteen years old when he went to look for a Bible, and someone told him to visit a pastor in another village. But the pastor told him he had only one Bible and he would not give it away. "If you want a Bible you have to pray and fast for it," he told the young boy.

So Brother Yun decided he would eat nothing but a bowl of rice a day until he got a Bible. This went on for one hundred days! Around that time he had a vision that someone gave him a parcel, a loaf of bread. When he woke up, he heard a knock on the door. He ran down to open it, and sure enough, there was someone standing there with a parcel. "We have a bread feast to give you," the stranger said. When he opened it, it was a Bible.

Brother Yun was so excited to have a Bible that he started reading it immediately. After reading it all he started to memorise the Gospel of Matthew. Soon this sixteen-year-old was going around all the local villages, preaching about Jesus and reciting the whole of Matthew to his audience.

As I read Yun's story, my hunger for God and his Word kept growing, and I started to pray and fast more. I wanted to experience God like that in my own life.

Another story that deeply impacted me was that of Hudson Taylor. He was still a teenager when he asked God to send him as a missionary to China. He was so filled with passion and vision from God, he wrote to his mother: "I cannot describe how I long to be a missionary, to carry the Glad Tidings to poor, perishing sinners, to spend and be spent for Him who died for me! . . . Think, Mother, of twelve millions – a number so great that it is impossible to realize – yes, twelve million souls in China, every year, passing without God and without hope into eternity".[3]

As I read about the passion and dedication Hudson Taylor had for China, I asked God to give me the same heart for the Global Youth Culture. And that's how I see this. There are lots of unreached people groups in the world. Over the history of missions waves of missionaries have reached different nations and people groups. But there is one unreached culture right now that is rapidly becoming, if it isn't already, the largest in the world. My hope through this book is to raise the awareness of the huge spiritual need of this generation and the call of God for a new missionary movement to lift up the Cross in this secular society.

After saving enough, my wife and I spent a year at All Nations getting some important training for missions. During that time, we asked God for direction for where we should go next. And as in other times, the vision came. At the end of 2009, we moved to São Paulo, Brazil, to help develop Steiger and reach the youth culture in one of the largest cities in the world.

7

Know the Scene

It was hard to know where to start, having just moved into a crowded central neighbourhood of an urban jungle boasting 20 million inhabitants. First on our list was to find out where the São Paulo youth scene happened. We went to the hip clubbing area of Rua Augusta, off Avenida Paulista. We visited the clubs and bars, met new people, and even filmed some interviews. (We often found people would open up even more if there was a camera.) This was a great time of building new friendships and getting to know the scene. This combined with daily times of prayer gave birth to a series of new ideas and vision for projects we were to develop over the next five years.

We joined forces with Sandro Baggio, who I mentioned before. He was the founder of Steiger in Brazil and also pastor and founder of Projeto 242, a very creative and dynamic church in the centre of São Paulo. The church gave us our first home, a small flat on the top floor of the church building.

One of our first projects was a band called Alegorica based on what we had learned spending years touring around the world with No Longer Music. We met for prayer with a group of actors and musicians from Projeto 242 and started working on a concept for a show that would portray the death and resurrection of Jesus in a language that young people in Brazil could understand.

Soon we were playing gigs in any bar or club that would have us. One of the first places we played was Luar Rock Bar on the northern outskirts of São Paulo. The place looked like an old bomb shelter. It was covered in graffiti from floor to ceiling and the toilet was a hole in the backyard. It consisted of two spaces. Inside was the stage, which was just a small platform about fifteen centimetres higher than the rest of the room. The ceiling was so low people regularly hit their heads during mosh pits. Outside was a dark yard, also covered in graffiti, that most people seemed to use for smoking weed and making out. Being bi-sexual was the most recent trend, so there were all sorts of things going on in that backyard. One of the bands that regularly played there was an all-girl punk-rock-protest band that was known for playing topless.

At the beginning, we tried to keep our set short and simple, but right from the start we wanted to show the cross and clearly preach Jesus anywhere we went. So near the end of our set, our actress got on stage performing a passionate monolog about false freedom and a system that oppresses us, which somehow quickly flowed into me representing Jesus and dying on the cross so she could be free again. At the end, I gave a short message and invited people to the front of the club to talk if they wanted to know more. We started doing gigs like this regularly, going to clubs all around the city. People responded every time, coming over to receive prayer and to talk.

Sandro's church, Projeto 242, was an easy place to invite people to once they were interested in knowing more. One time I was speaking about how Che Guevara, the South American revolutionary, was nothing like the true revolution that Jesus could bring. We'd advertised it on Facebook I noticed some skinny-jeaned dudes standing in the back of the meeting who I didn't recognise, so I went over and introduced myself. We talked a bit. They were from a hardcore band from Guarulhos (a municipality near São Paulo). Moah, the lead singer of the band, found that theme interesting. He told me he liked my message. "We want to share this message in our band". Surprised, I asked them what church they were from, but they said they didn't go to a church. Moah explained that he thought the message about Jesus was powerful, but he didn't know much about it. He then asked me something every missionary wants to hear: "Could you teach me more about Jesus?" I jumped on this exciting opportunity and suggested we start a Bible study together. So they invited me to their rehearsal space.

That next week I was on the bus to Guarulhos, heading to their band practice. They met in this tiny, smelly room with no windows, which always seemed to be packed with their friends watching the rehearsal. After practise, Moah handed me the microphone and said, "preach"! I didn't expect this, so I hadn't prepared anything. I just started talking about what it meant to follow Jesus. When I finished, he told me it was good and asked if I could come again the following week.

Soon we moved our Bible study to a local bar to have more space. Each week there were ten to fifteen of us sitting around the bar tables reading and discussing the gospel. It was amazing to read through the life of Jesus with these guys, some of whom had never read the Bible or heard the stories before. Soon many of them got baptised and a couple years later they even ended up at our mission training centre in Germany.

Right from day one they were sharing their faith from the stage at their concerts every weekend and inviting their friends to our Bible study in the bar, which consequently was always full. The reason for all this was that these guys were "scene guys". They knew everyone. When they decided to follow Jesus, they didn't leave their friends behind. They didn't stop being part of the scene. They just became salt and light where Jesus placed them. They used the influence they had on stage to speak truth, and they showed what it meant to follow Jesus in their relationships. They were missionaries from day one.

Step Outside the Church Walls

We need to realise that there is a cultural gap between the church and the Global Youth Culture. In what seems a contradiction, the church is out of touch with the global culture while at the same time greatly influenced by it, often taking on values and perspectives contrary to the Christian faith. This is the opposite to how Jesus lived. Jesus was keenly in tune with the culture around him, in relationship with many who deeply differed in mindset and belief, and yet he did not bow down to the predominant cultural and religious influence of the time. Instead, he challenged the Jewish culture and mindset. Starting from the common ground of the Jewish scriptures, he called even the most respected religious leaders to be born again. When Peter, and later Paul, went to the Gentiles, they had to let go of their cultural trappings and adhere to new cultural paradigms in order to make the gospel real to their listeners and have real transformational power in that new context. When Hudson Taylor went to China, he lived and dressed like the rural Chinese to avoid the distraction of his Western clothing and culture, allowing him to preach the Good News to a more attentive audience. Bridging cultural gaps has always been at the core of the biblical and historical missions movement.

In the past, missions meant going to a distant land to learn a new language, eat strange food, and adapt to foreign cultures, but the largest mission field today are the very cities in which we live. We need to practice the same flexibility and cultural adaptability to share Jesus in our own neighbourhood in this time when our faith has been pushed to the margins and is now seen as strange and alien to the culture around us. We need to make the same effort of getting to know the culture in which we now live, so we can be influencers rather than negatively influenced.

The first step is recognising that we should be talking about the Global Youth Culture in the first person. This affects us all. It's not us versus them, the church versus the world. Globalism, consumerism, secular humanism, and all its consequences have deeply infiltrated the church.

The influence of relativism has caused a widespread dualism in the Western church, with a lot of members living double lives, one on Sunday and another the rest of the week. Faced with scepticism and a "post-truth" environment, many have struggled to keep the faith, wondering if they really need to take it as seriously as their pastor tells them to. Francis Schaeffer pointed out, relativism even affected our theology, creating strings of liberal theology that fit much more neatly into the secular humanist worldview rather than a biblical one.

Consumerism has probably taken the largest toll on the church culture. Focused on entertainment more than anything else, the showbiz of the church service tries to compete with the entertainment industry for people's attention. This has created a superficial, self-centred faith that has us constantly searching for the next spiritual experience in the next conference and shopping for the ideal church to meet our needs.

Just as consumerism leads to fragmented relationships and a loss of identity in the Global Youth Culture, so too the church has often lost its sense of community and finds itself in an identity crisis. This fast-moving, no-commitment generation has formed churches that are more like social clubs with loosely affiliated visitors than a family of members deeply committed to each other as described in Acts.

Much of the church has lost its identity and so struggles to know how to stand in a society constantly moving and changing. We have no voice because we don't know what to say. We're not in the debate because we've forgotten what our message is.

While under the influence of the global culture, we have somehow simultaneously alienated ourselves and become irrelevant to a growing unchurched generation. In fear of losing ourselves in this state of unease and identity crisis, we have chosen to hide in a church ghetto. The very young people who are most in need of the gospel are seen as dangerous influencers who might infect the existing members. Bogged down with unnecessary church culture, we struggle to connect with the world around us, to the extent that our most earnest attempts of evangelism can't breach the walls of the church and fail to have any real reach in the global scene.

How can we revert this situation? How can we fulfil Jesus' calling to go to all the earth, to go to the Global Youth Culture, and make disciples?

Only by spending time again at the feet of Jesus can we remember who we are and find our identity and purpose again. And when we remember our calling, we can pray, as the church in Acts did, that God would give us boldness that we might step outside the church walls and be salt and light.

That's what Jesus taught us. He never intended us to hide in church buildings, alienating ourselves in search of holiness. He cried out to the Father, "My prayer is not that you take them out of the world but that you protect them from the evil one. . . . I have sent them into the world" (John 17:15, 18).

Jesus' teaching on salt and light gives us the perfect balance to be in the world yet not of it. He calls us "the salt of the earth" (Matt. 5:13). Salt was used to preserve food and to give it taste. It preserves the goodness of the food and makes it better. To be salt means to be distinct. Then he says, "you are the light of the world" (Matt. 5:14). He talks about a town on a hill that all can see and a lamp placed high on a stand to illuminate the room. The light must shine, it must be seen by all. To be light means to be influential.

Jesus calls us to be distinct and influential. The problem is that sometimes we, the church, are too salty. We're so salty that no one can eat the food. We're so different that no one can understand us; we seem alien to the world around us. In fear of the world, we shut ourselves up in the ghetto and lose our relevance; we have no influence. In other cases, we fall to the other extreme. We become the pop church, the hip church, with an influential voice. Our light shines bright, but we have lost our saltiness. We become the same as the world around us, losing our values and identity, losing our distinctness, our focus on the good news of Jesus. This commercial Christianity is filled with quick solutions and easy answers but has no power. Some reject it as just another product on offer, while others consume it but experience no real change. We need to stop offering a cheap Christianity to a generation that is tired of consumerism. We need to leave the ghetto and preach again the genuine and radical message of Jesus.

Jesus has called us to be both salt and light, to be different and influential, to be relevant, involved, and engaged in the global culture, yet without losing our identity in Him. He has called us to be the voice of truth, lifting up the cross and proclaiming a living Saviour. That's where the power is. That's what people are looking for.

Jesus Knew the Scene

Sometimes we try to come up with cool strategies to reach people, but we don't take the time to get to know them. Jesus knew the scene. He spent all his time meeting people, having meals with them, listening to them, and caring for and healing them. As a result, he gained their respect and esteem, and he was able to communicate in a way they could understand.

Jesus lived during a challenging time and place in history. The region in which he walked, taught, and ministered was politically charged, culturally diverse, and marked by social inequality. The Jewish people faced oppression living under the Roman superpower. Some people fought back, some became more isolated in their religious nationalism, and others just struggling to survive under the heavy taxation system. In general, people were longing for change; they were looking for someone to follow, and there were many options—various political parties, religious groups, and rebel movements—each with their own message. Perhaps in some ways it was not too far from our reality today.

It was in this context that Jesus came, declaring the kingdom of God was near. He didn't have a powerful party behind him, big financial investors, or an easy platform from which to speak. He started in the smallest and poorest neighbourhoods, meeting people, caring for people, and preaching a clear and bold message, often through a creative and powerful art form: parables. I want to emphasise these three ways in which Jesus engaged in the scene to minister to people: He spent time with people investing in relationships. He responded to immediate and real-life questions. And he communicated creatively through stories and parables, a way they could understand.

That first activity seems to be the one Jesus spent the most time on. Throughout the Gospel narratives, Jesus was walking the streets and meeting people. Sometimes He was inviting Himself to people's homes, sometimes having intense one-on-one conversations, sometimes sharing with a group or a crowd of thousands. In all these situations, He gave himself completely to people, engaging them with His full attention and energy until He was exhausted. He was able to connect with people from all different walks of life. Even in His closest circle of followers there were people from very different backgrounds: fishermen, a tax collector, and a political activist. He gave the poor high priority, but he also spent time with the rich, loving them the same. He spent time with the political class and the religious leaders. Even the Pharisees, who we often see as the bad guys, spent a lot of time around Jesus engaging Him in deep debates. His main concern was with people's hearts. He would look people in the eye and ask them piercing questions, speaking directly to their most intimate fears and desires.

Jesus was constantly involved in people's lives. He responded to people's questions and needs. His ministry was marked by miracles of healing, setting people free from evil spirits, and providing material needs. On one hand, Jesus was performing miracles as evidence that he was sent by God. But on the other hand He was simply responding out of compassion to people's needs. Jesus was moved by compassion (Matt. 9:36).

Jesus also confronted oppressive religious and socio-political structures and called together a new community to demonstrate alternative values, and he did all with non-violence and selflessness. He opposed religious elitism (Matt. 23:25), answered political questions like whether or not to pay taxes (Mark 12:17), forgave and fellowshipped with sinners, and even staged a protest when he cleansed the temple (Luke 19).

Lastly, Jesus communicated creatively in a way people could understand. This point is particularly relevant when thinking about our context of youth culture. Jesus' parables were in tune with the storytelling culture of the time and communicated truth in a relevant way. More than a strategy, it was a natural result of spending time with people and knowing the culture.

As we respond to God's calling, to go into the world and to be salt and light, we can look to Jesus' example as our best missionary model. He knew the scene. He spent time with people, built real relationships, and responded to their needs and questions; he communicated creatively and relevantly.

We often use art and music to share the good news with the Global Youth Culture. They are powerful tools, not only to communicate but as entrees into the cultural scene and people's lives. That's why many of the following examples circle around art and cultural events. But it's also important to emphasise here that you don't have to be an artist to reach Global Youth. Knowing the scene, building relationships, and sharing the truth with people can be done in many ways. It is the heart for people and the willingness to go to them that will make us effective in changing the world today.

The Art that Jesus Mastered

Jesus grew up in a storytelling culture. The Greeks told fables, and the Jewish rabbis spoke in *mashal*, a very common oral and literary art form used when teaching the Torah. Storytelling was possibly the most well-known and appreciated art form of that time, and it is still very present in Middle Eastern culture and tradition today.

This is precisely the medium of artistic expression that Jesus chose to use. The word *parable* is the Greek translation of the Hebrew word *mashal*, and parables were true works of art. They captured the imagination of the hearers with their intriguing characters and though-provoking twists and lessons.

Although parables were not Jesus' invention, he was a master of them – arguably the best there has ever been! Not only did he choose this popular art form to communicate his message, He was also involved in its scene - repeating and interacting with the parables already well known among his Jewish audience. Jesus knew the *mashal*, and he respected its rules and common formulas. The rabbinic tradition tended to start a parable with the introductory question and answer: "Unto what is the matter like? It is like . . .", a pattern Jesus often followed. Similarly, a parable would conclude with the expression "even so" or "likewise", and Jesus adopted these terms as well.

Some of Jesus' parables are practically "covers" of stories other rabbis had already told. But even in the ones He repeated from the existing oral tradition, Jesus often threw a twist or challenge that brought across his bold message of the kingdom to come and that revealed his true nature. Check out this rabbinic parable:

> A person in whom there are good deeds and who has studied the Torah extensively, what is he like? A man who builds first [of] stones and then afterwards [of] mud bricks. Even if a large quantity of water were to collect beside the stones, it would not destroy them. But a person in whom there are no good deeds, though he has studied Torah, what is he like? A man who builds first [of] mud bricks and then afterwards [of] stones. Even if only a little water collects, it immediately undermines them.[1]

Do you feel like you've heard it before? Jesus did covers! This is very similar to one of Jesus' well-known parables about the man who builds his house on the sand compared to the one who builds on the rock. There is one small yet monumental difference. All the other rabbis spoke of knowing and doing the words of Torah, but Jesus introduced his account with the words, "A person who hears these words of mine and does them". No rabbi, being a mere man, would ever have referred to his own words in such way when addressing a

Jewish audience. Only God himself spoke in this way. This is the equivalent of Jesus playing a cover of a well-known song and adding a twist at the end to make his audience stop and think. Through this artistic form of storytelling, Jesus revealed Himself as the promised Messiah, as God Himself.

Rabbinic parables tended to reinforce conventional wisdom or societal norms. Jesus, however, constantly challenged the status quo. When telling the story of the good Samaritan, his listeners would certainly have identified with the Jerusalem-Jericho road and its dangers, and most would also have smiled at the cynical portrayal of the religious elite passing by. The Samaritan coming in as the hero of the story, though, would have been a powerful and provocative challenge to all.

In this storytelling culture, Jesus' parables were extremely relevant. The poor, the farmers, the fishermen, and many others in society, all could identify with His stories. The religious class knew *mashal* well. He also spoke to the political scene and the powerful of the time through provocative illustrations. Jesus connected intimately to the scene on various levels, through an art form known and practised in his day. There's so much we can learn from him and apply to our own art today.

If you are an artist, have a band, or want to connect to the cultural scene, then make Jesus your example: He used a relevant art form to connect to the people, yet He did not submit to their thinking. Instead He told His own stories, intentionally provocative, to get them to think.

Jesus purposefully used his art to communicate truth. He never conformed to simply repeating or imitating what other rabbis were saying or doing.

He adapted his art form to each audience, making personal connections and playing off the audience's reactions.

Jesus was willing to discuss his parables after telling them, expound them when necessary.

His art was a part of his ministry but not its sum total; His purpose was much greater. Jesus cared about people: healing them, spending time with them, and preaching the truth to them. His medium of artistic expression came into play at different times, but it was only one tool of many. His art had a clear message and purpose, adding to the larger picture of His life and ministry.

Some of these points are especially poignant for us today in a relativistic culture that has taken upon itself to deconstruct art itself, calling for "art for art's sake" and pretending to have no message or refusing to ever explain a piece. Art always has a message. Having no message is a message. Don't be so arrogant as to close yourself up from your audience, refusing to share and explain your intent. Humility and vulnerability will go a long way to truly connect with your audience and make a real difference in the scene.

My prayer is that you would follow the footsteps of Jesus in your art.

Becoming All Things to the Scene

Stepping outside the church walls, knowing the scene, and seeking to be salt and light by being influential and distinct often presents dilemmas. When we think about reaching the culture, we need to ask ourselves a few questions. How should we live in this world today? What does it mean to be a follower of Jesus in the scene I'm already a part of? What can and can't we do? What is sinful and what is just cultural? As discussed before it seems that the church often falls into one of two extremes: either in our search for holiness we become isolated and alienated from the culture around us or we sell out to the culture and forget our values and identity as followers of Jesus. So how do we get this right?

In 1 Corinthians 9:22 Paul talks about "becoming all things to all men," and I've often heard this passage used to discuss the need for the church to adapt to the culture. Oftentimes a superficial interpretation of this is presented. We imagine Paul dressing up as a Greek person, pretending to be someone he wasn't in order to trick people into listening to him. So we imitate something we've observed in the art and culture around us in the hope that it will win us favour with the people we are trying to reach. I might think if I play hardcore music, all the hardcore kids will convert. If I dress up in black, the goths might listen to me. I like Slipknot, so I'll just make a Christian version of it.

Another mistake we make here is to think that Paul is saying he'll do anything to reach people in the sense that anything goes. We might think we can leave certain values or standards behind in the name of identifying with people. So we think we have to swear in our lyrics or drink beer and smoke a pipe so people will think we're cool. That's missing the point Paul is making.

In fact, it's the opposite. In 1 Corinthians 8 Paul talks about how eating meat offered to idols was confusing for new believers coming from the Greek cultural scene. He says that if it's a barrier for Greeks to know Jesus, he will never eat meat again. He then goes on to say that he's willing to remain single and never get paid for his missionary work if that will help him reach more people. He concludes by saying he has "become all things to all people" so that by all possible means he might save some (1 Cor. 9:22).

Paul was willing to let go of all his rights to connect with the scene and share Jesus with people. His was a life sacrificially shared with people, truly identifying with them and showing them what it means to follow Jesus. This was a deep and long-term commitment. With a servant attitude, he gave up everything and dedicated his life to the people God called him to. He wanted to show a Greek person what it meant to be a Greek person who follows Jesus.

The world doesn't need cheap imitations. It doesn't need a church that puts on a costume to connect with the culture, or people leaving their Christian values and identity behind in the name of identifying with the scene. The scene needs strong and genuine followers of Jesus, boldly modelling what it means to follow Jesus. What does a hardcore band in São Paulo that follows Jesus look like? What does a London high street banker who follows Jesus look like? What does a graphic designer in New York who follows Jesus look like? The scene needs Christians who are authentic, connected, influential, and passionate for the gospel willing to dedicate their lives and let go of their rights to help this generation meet Jesus.

For us this meant walking together with the guys from the hard-core band in Guarulhos. It meant playing in some rough clubs; it meant long bus rides to meet in their small rehearsal room; and eventually it meant us moving with our two-year-old son to Guarulhos and renting a community house with eight of the guys and girls who were now growing fast in their faith.

Manifeste

Once we had our band Alegorica up and going, with regular gigs in clubs around São Paulo and occasionally traveling to other cities, and the Bible study was growing in Guarulhos with Moah and the crew from his band No More Lies, we started organising some events together. The church Projeto 242 included many artists, bands, and other creative types like Angelo and Aline, who ran their own alternative film production collective. There was a lot of potential to organise interesting events and engage in the cultural scene of the city.

We started a movement called Manifeste. The concept was to organise regular events in different locations that would mix various art forms and create common ground with non-Christian artists and the scene in general. We would put together concerts with different styles of music and at the same time have an art or photography exhibition, a book stall with independent "zines", film viewings and discussions, and other things all in the same event. The majority of the artists performing weren't Christians, but we would have one or two key Christian artists there to share a message. The events were completely for the general audience, not the church. But at every event, we would share a clear and bold message about Jesus.

One time, Moah got a connection with an influential cultural venue in the centre of São Paulo. This was mid 2014, the year after the violent protests against bus and metro fare hikes. The guys running the venue had also been mobilisers in the protests and riots that had happened in São Paulo, and there were rumours that some of them were part of the infamous "black-blocs", a group who carried out acts of vandalism and violence during the protests. They had heard about some of our Manifeste events and invited us to use their place for a special edition. They had a three-floor building and offered us two floors. (The other floor was for an exhibition promoting the legalisation of cannabis.) We jumped at the opportunity, knowing that this was exactly the kind of place where we wanted to be. It would mean sharing the good news where it had not been shared before.

We put together a line-up with four or five bands, an art exhibition, and a film raising awareness about human trafficking. Our band, Alegorica, would play at a key time to share Jesus with the most people possible. In the run up to the event, various people came to me with concerns about us preaching there. "Luke you can't preach there; these are black-bloc guys. Just do a chilled event and build relationships". But we knew God had given us this opportunity for a reason, and we were committed to telling people the truth.

When the day came, the venue was packed, as it was also during a city-wide cultural event, and there was no entrance fee. We set up and then gathered to pray in a backstage area. As it was every time, I was nervous and praying hard God would help me to know what to say. We showed the dramatisation of the crucifixion and resurrection of

Jesus, and I ended with a clear message inviting people to meet Jesus. I told those who responded to the message to come to the backstage room and around twenty people showed up. We led people in prayer and the band shared stories. Then one girl from the audience asked to share. She explained how she had seen our show the year before in a club and had met Jesus. "I knew about God before, but I had forgotten him. It was like he went into the club after me. He never gave up on me". This was a powerful testimony to the people who were just then responding to the same message.

At the end of the event, one of the venue managers, the political activist type, a Rastafarian with long dreadlocks, went over to Moah and Angelo. He thanked us for the event and asked if we'd be interested in an ongoing arrangement for regular events there.

There are no closed doors for the gospel. If we become deeply involved in the scene, investing in relationships and at the same time boldly sharing the message of the cross, there is no heart too hard and no place too difficult.

Go to Them

To reiterate the point, we need to know the scene, engage in it, be part of it, and communicate relevantly in context. But how do we do this? How do we start?

Just as we did in the first year in São Paulo, when we start new initiatives in a city we follow two steps: one, we spend lots of time in prayer asking God for his vision and two we build relationships by going where people are: events, clubs, festivals, wherever the scene is happening.

When we started evangelistic efforts with the students at the Steiger Mission School (SMS) in Germany, we hit the hip streets of Neustadt in Dresden. Just walking down Alaunstrasse you get a sense of the diverse, young family–orientated, artistic, hipster scene there. The street art speaks loudly, the venues define a cultural identity, and the walls are covered in posters of interesting events, alternative theatres, concerts, parties, and more. One of the first things we ask our students to do is go to some of these venues and events and observe, get to know people, introduce yourself, and make new connections. One time a street artist from Brazil attending the SMS walked straight into the local graffiti store and introduced himself. He got to know various people hanging out there, and before he knew it he was invited by some local artists to paint some walls officially allocated for graffiti artwork in a nearby square.

When we started the café in the London area, one of the first things we did was go with the team to the parks where young people were hanging out drinking and just start talking to them and inviting them over to the party I described in chapter 1. This may mean stepping outside of your comfort zone and meeting people different to your usual social circle. But as you seek Jesus for boldness and patience, this will lead to interesting new relationships and open doors to connect with the scene. Doing this will take time, and that's not a bad thing. It will open the doors to long-term relationships and bigger opportunities to share the gospel in a relevant way.

Once you're out there meeting people and getting to know the scene, ask God for a vision and ideas of how to share the gospel and lead people to Jesus. When David and his team started out in Amsterdam in the eighties, they spent time visiting the punk clubs. It was during that time that God inspired David with the vision for No Longer Music. Each situation can call for a different approach, so asking God for his vision in each specific context is important. But it's important to be ready to obey when God gives you a vision. This means taking that step of faith, being bold, and starting with what we have. At this point, we don't need to wait until we have the perfect idea or the perfect artistic tool or all the resources. I've found that God often uses the simplest things, especially at the beginning. He honours our steps of obedience. Maybe that means just going and talking to people about Jesus in a club or offering prayer on the streets. Maybe it means starting to play gigs in the local bar with those first three or four songs. Whatever it is, don't wait. Pray and then act.

Another thing we've often prayed for is that God would lead us to meet some key influencers in the scene. I've frequently seen God use a key person to open the doors for big opportunities for the gospel. Meeting Moah and his band was crucial to seeing the work unfold in Guarulhos. The Bible study happened because he invited his friends and one thing led to another. When we started to see the café in London fill up with people, it was mainly due to a few of those key influencers deciding to go and inviting all the rest. I often call these "scene guys or girls". Their gift is relational. They are good at networking in the scene. They know everyone. They know the best clubs and venues; they know what's happening, what bands and artists are around. They are the best people to organise shows, events, Bible studies, or whatever God puts on your heart because they are natural leaders in that scene. Ask God to lead you to that key scene guy or girl.

So summarising, I've suggested four practical steps I believe are important to reach the scene:

1. Pray for God's vision and observe the scene (find out what's happening and what the scene is like).

2. Build real and long-term relationships with people.

3. Pray for and seek out key influencers in the scene, the scene guy or girl.

4. Don't wait to act, to start something in partnership with those key people.

Once you've built relationships and understand what's happening in the city and neighbourhood God has called you to, your efforts in evangelism and discipleship will tend to be so much more relevant and impactful. If you keep at it for the long term, God can use you in amazing ways and the work can grow beyond our expectations.

8

Speak the Truth

Jesus called us to be salt and light—distinct and influential—to the world. So it's not enough to just be part of the scene and have good relationships, we need to tell people the truth. That's what we were trying to do with the band Alegorica.

As I said before, it all started with a small group of us getting together to pray and think about how we could communicate the message of Jesus to the São Paulo scene. We decided we would play psycho-electro-scream rock. (Don't try googleing that; I don't think it's a thing.) Most of our team were from Projeto 242 church, such as Hudson and Dalila, a creative couple who had a cool combination of being innovative musicians and at the same time good at helping people grow in their faith. We had a professional actress called Veronica, an ex-Buddhist contemporary dancer called Nitiren, and David, our Brazilian-Korean visual artist designing our scenography and look.

After playing a few gigs with the first five songs we wrote, and a very basic dramatisation of the death and resurrection of Jesus, I decided we needed to take it to the next level. I called Adam, our prop builder, a Polish Steiger volunteer who came to work with us in São Paulo for a year and told him we needed to build a cage. He came to the church yard, where I had started gathering materials. "What's it for?" he asked.

"During the crucifixion I want to be hanging two meters off the floor with chains and hooks", I explained. Adam just laughed and shook his head. "I'm serious," I went on. "We need to show how dramatic the cross is, in a contemporary way. We need to lift up the cross in the clubs". So we spent the week creating a suspended "crucifixion" special effect.

Our set and lyrics dealt with various issues that people in São Paulo were talking about, like consumerism, relationships, sex, abortion, and spirituality. A girl dramatised a suicide attempt. I would try to stop her, and the band would grab me, hang me up by the hooks and chains with my arms stretched out as if on a cross. One band member would then kill me with a knife and then slowly lower my body to the ground. Then, in a sombre atmosphere, they would cover my body with a white cloth. As the music kicked back in, we had some dramatic lighting effects going on as I would rise up to show the resurrection. As I faced the girl, now curled on the stage, I would tell her "Don't believe the lies anymore. It's time to meet the ultimate life force. He has always been by your side. He wants to give you true freedom. He loves you unconditionally. His name . . . (the band goes quiet) is Jesus". His name was the last word of the performance, and we'd leave people hanging on that name.

Some of those lines were from the No Longer Music concert. I'd seen God's power around the world as we clearly proclaimed that message in No Longer Music, and that was what we wanted to see happen in Brazil and wherever God would take Alegorica. We wanted people to see the character of Jesus, and how he really cared about them. Too many people today have a negative idea of God. They see an empty and superficial religiosity, and they think God is far away and irrelevant to their lives. But the truth is He loves them, and His heart breaks for them. Often people would come up to us after the show and say, "I've never thought about Jesus like that before".

We played as often as we could in Brazil, and soon we got the chance to travel to some unexpected corners of the world.

Murmansk

Our first tour outside Brazil with Alegorica was about as far away as you could go. After the long flight from Brazil to Helsinki airport, we took a ten-hour bus ride to northern Finland. Then we crossed the border into Russia. Our bus broke down, so we had to spend the night in a forest by the road with nothing to eat but cold leftover reindeer pizza. The next day, after we got the bus repaired, we had another eight-hour drive to Murmansk. The team was exhausted. .

On the way, I asked the organiser what kind of venue we were playing, and he said, "I have no respect for this place. It is a place of murderers, where they have fights every night". So we were very encouraged. Because of the delay on the road, we arrived late. With no time to rest, we headed straight to the venue. When we got there, the owner, who looked like a mafia boss, greeted us. "I heard you're a Christian band. I want you to know I'm an atheist". He also said our show was booked for too early in the evening, and people would only arrive after the show. Gathering in the car park, we prayed with the team that God would bring people. While praying we had the idea to ask the club owner to let us play twice. To our surprise, he agreed.

During the show the place was full, and people seemed to like the music. But a group of guys at the front was mocking the act all the time. Near the end I was nervous, praying hard in between songs. "God this is Russia," I prayed silently. "I don't think I can preach here like we do back in Brazil". But as often happens when I'm praying, I sensed God encouraging me to be bold. As I gave a message, the guys who had been mocking went quiet and became serious. I invited people forward, and one of those guys was the first to come. Others followed and people at the bar started to clap. We invited those who responded backstage and the room was filled with around forty people wanting to hear more.

A journalist came into the back of the room and asked to do an interview. I explained that we wanted to talk with the people, but that she could listen. So she sat and wrote down everything we were saying. I explained more about following Jesus. The people listened intently, and then we led people in prayer to receive Jesus. At this point the journalist was in tears. She also surrendered her life to Jesus. We asked if anyone had questions, and one girl raised her hand. "Why are you doing this here in this club? You should be sharing this message in the main square for everyone to hear. Nobody has ever told me the things you have about God".

The next day we went to church in Murmansk. It was a small gathering of people, mostly over sixty years old. As we sat there, suddenly a group of four young people from the club where we had played walked into the back of the small meeting room. One of them went and sat next to an older lady, who then started to cry. I asked the pastor, who was sitting next to me, whether they knew each other. "That's her son," he explained. "She's been praying for him to come back to church for years". The young girl who had asked us why we weren't in the public square proclaiming the good news for all to hear also showed up.

Lifting Up the Cross Outside the Church

It's awesome being part of God's family, the church, and experiencing His power in church meetings when we worship and hear the teaching of the Word. But our passion is to see God moving outside the church, on the streets, in the clubs, at festivals, and in all the places where people need to hear the truth. The Global Youth Culture needs the chance to meet Jesus and hear how He defeated death and opened the way to God for everyone. When this message is preached in places where people have never heard it, God moves with power.

One time I toured in Santiago, Chile, with No Longer Music. Our hosts were a well-known secular heavy metal band from Santiago. They organised various concerts for us where we were able to share Jesus around their city. We played in clubs where people were shooting up and vomiting all over the toilets. But God was moving powerfully.

In one show, Cocke, the guitar player of the host band was working the soundboard. We had managed to find a local Christian translator to translate the message in the show, but he wasn't doing a very good job. As we were lifting up the cross, suddenly Cocke grabs a microphone in the back and starts passionately translating the message.

At the end of the show, he came over to us shaking. "I'm really sorry, I don't know why I did that".

"Don't worry about it, Cocke. It sounded great!" we replied.

He explained that he hadn't intended to take over the translation, but he had suddenly felt the urge to. He said the feeling was so strong that it was as if he would vomit if he didn't shout out the words. "I don't know what was going on, but it felt like I was the voice of God in Spanish! What's happening to me?" he asked, still shaking.

We explained that it was the Spirit of God moving through him.

We invited him to come to church with us the next day. David Pierce was preaching and when he ended, he invited people to come forward to receive Jesus. Cocke was the first person down front on his knees. We gathered around to pray for him. He was sobbing and shaking, confessing his sins and asking for forgiveness. Later he explained that he felt like a hand was coming into his chest and pulling bad things out. He was a changed man.

He went everywhere with us and participated in all our team prayer times and Bible studies. When we left Chile to go on tour to Brazil, Cocke came with us. I met with him daily to read through the gospel and teach him more about Jesus. Eventually, we all left the tour, and he went back to Santiago. But he was completely sold out for Jesus. He found a small traditional Pentecostal church in his neighbourhood, walked in, and sat down. At first, the congregation wasn't sure what to make of him or his tattoos and dreadlocks. But he stuck to it, knowing those were his new brothers and sisters. In the following years, he also toured with NLM, and was a bold evangelist for the gospel.

Whether it be South America, the Middle East, or Europe, we have seen God move powerfully, drawing people to himself when we are willing to proclaim the message of the cross in a clear and relevant way. Often, after shows people will come up and say things like, "I'm not usually into Jesus or religious stuff, but this made me think again" or "I'd never thought about Jesus in this way". Most people in the Global Youth Culture have the wrong idea about Jesus, so we need to knock down those preconceived ideas. When people get the chance to meet the real Jesus and truly understand who he is and what he has done, they want to know Him.

More than anything else, to reach the Global Youth Culture for Jesus, we need to proclaim the truth. And as we do, we need to remember the gospel truth is powerful, relevant, provocative, and it must be clear.

Powerful Truth

It is easy to be intimidated by the global predominant worldview. Our message appears foolish to this relativistic culture. The apostle Paul faced all kinds of opposition to the message about Jesus, yet he explains it is God's plan to show his power:

> For the message of the cross is foolishness to those who are perishing, but to us who are being saved it is the power of God. For it is written:
>
> "I will destroy the wisdom of the wise; the intelligence of the intelligent I will frustrate".
>
> Where is the wise person? Where is the teacher of the law? Where is the philosopher of this age? Has not God made foolish the wisdom of the world? For since in the wisdom of God the world through its wisdom did not know him, God was

pleased through the foolishness of what was preached to save those who believe. Jews demand signs and Greeks look for wisdom, but we preach Christ crucified: a stumbling block to Jews and foolishness to Gentiles, but to those whom God has called, both Jews and Greeks, Christ the power of God and the wisdom of God. For the foolishness of God is wiser than human wisdom, and the weakness of God is stronger than human strength. (1 Corinthians 1:18-25)

The Global Youth Culture might be steeped in relativism, but there is a deep spiritual hunger. We can look at the mindset around us and the apathy towards Christianity and be fearful to speak, afraid to offend. But if we show people who Jesus really is, and show the cross, then the power of God moves and people want to know Him.

One time we organised a Manifeste event at a skate park on the outskirts of São Paulo. We were going to play with a very influential band in the São Paulo rock scene. The lead singer was a preacher. But he didn't preach the good news about Jesus, he taught a humanistic worldview: "Believe in whatever you want, just believe in something. Believe in yourself".

The night before we were going to play, I had a dream. I saw this band playing in front of hundreds of people who were listening to their message. There was a weird New Age spiritual vibe, and people were meditating and even levitating. It felt overwhelming, powerful, and evil. I woke up feeling afraid. "God, how can I talk about you in this environment. They all know the Christian message, and they think it's lame. They think we're fanatics or something".

When we got to the skate park, I gathered my band together and told them about my dream. We prayed that God would move with power when we preached the message and that the other band would meet Jesus that day.

As the other band played the singer went on passionate rants in between every song. "I know you're all fighting for good. Believe in your potential. We're not standing under any religious banner here; just believe in what's good". I expected that was a jab at us since they knew we were Christians.

We played after them. As we finished our portrayal of the cross, I stood at the edge of the stage and explained as clearly as I could that no matter how hard we tried, we can't make the world a better place in our own strength. "Jesus came to defeat the death inside of us by defeating death on the cross. He can clean you and change you from the inside out. But you have to surrender to him. If you want to know Jesus, come over to the side of the stage so we can pray with you".

We stepped off to the side of the stage. Around fifty people came forward. To my excitement I saw three members of the other band standing in the front of the line, including the lead singer. We led people in a prayer to receive Jesus. Afterward the singer spoke to one of our team members. "I feel like I've been looking for something for a long time, and I've found it today".

The foolishness of God is wiser than human wisdom. As the message is preached, God draws even the hardest hearts to himself. He is irresistible. I get so excited seeing the different ways God reveals himself, his power, and his reality.

One time we played in a club in São Paulo called Hangar 110. After the show I talked to a guy called Renan who was clearly moved and very aware of God's presence in the club. The night before he dreamed he was in a cage and that evil was all around him. He felt trapped. The following morning, he visited a friend and told her about his dream. Then they went together to the concert. They watched the Alegorica performance with the cage and the theme of being trapped, ending with the clear message that Jesus sets us free through his death and resurrection. As they stood watching, Renan's friend grabbed him by the arm and in tears said, "your dream!"

After we talked, I prayed with him. "It's clear to me now that there is a way out. I want to thank I don't know who for this message". Later that day he posted on Facebook: "Thank you, God, for the message I heard at the show". Renan was drawn to Jesus after God prepared him for the message of the show through a dream.

The youth today need to experience the power of God. This generation that no longer accepts absolute truth, needs signs to validate the message. It's been exciting to observe more believers pray boldly for healing in a fresh movement of spontaneous street evangelism all around the world. God is revealing himself in a supernatural way to my generation. And the greatest miracle of all is when God opens the eyes of those who don't know him, as the message of the good news is preached, and the cross is lifted up.

Personal experience is so important to this global generation. Jesus called us to make disciples (Matt. 28:19), and that starts with a personal encounter with Him. Young people need to experience the power and reality of God in whichever way God chooses to reveal himself.

Subversive Truth

Colossians describes in beautiful detail the inherent power of the cross, reminding us of what happens when we boldly proclaim this truth. It describes the cross as the climax of a cosmic battle, the most subversive act in history and the pivotal moment of God's revolution.

The believers in Colossae were being influenced by ideas and philosophies that were distracting them from the centrality and sufficiency of Christ. So Paul wrote to the Colossians to bring them back to an exclusive faith in Christ. He reminded the Colossians who Jesus really is, of His supreme power, his spiritual authority, and that his sacrificial act on the cross is all they need to have the fullness of life.

As Paul points to the amazing power and authority of Jesus, he describes an exciting drama of a battle between Christ and the visible and invisible powers and authorities of this world:

> When you were dead in your sins and in the uncircumcision of your flesh, God made you alive with Christ. He forgave us all our sins, having canceled the charge of our legal indebtedness, which stood against us and condemned us; he has taken it away, nailing it to the cross. And having disarmed the powers and authorities, he made a public spectacle of them, triumphing over them by the cross. (Col. 2:13-15).

In chapter 1, Paul had already explained that Jesus is Creator and Lord and that he is victorious over all through the most subversive and revolutionary act in history: his death and resurrection. And now, in chapter 2, Paul describes three enemies defeated at the cross: an invisible spiritual enemy, a visible human system (Col. 2:15) and our own sin (Col. 2:11-14). We know he refers to both visible and invisible "powers and authorities" because that's how he describes them in the previous chapter (Col. 1:15).

Both in verses 11 and 15 of chapter 2, Paul uses a similar Greek term, which in English could be translated "disarm". Verse 11 tells us our sinful self was "put off" and verse 15 describes how Jesus "disarmed the powers and authorities" in his work on the cross. It means we are free from something that oppresses us. To disarm the enemy means to take away his power. This is the subversive act of the cross.

A subversive act is a provocative act, that disturbs the order and brings change. This is God turning everything upside down. The unforgivable is forgiven, oppressive power is disarmed, the last will be the first, pain becomes peace, and sadness becomes joy.

The first enemy defeated at the cross is the Devil. The Bible talks about an enemy—Satan—who is evil and tempts us to evil, and it talks of a spiritual world that affects us. The apostle Peter tells us to "Be alert and sober minded. Your enemy the devil prowls around like a roaring lion looking for someone to devour" (1 Pet. 5:8). On the cross Jesus exposed the Devil and unmasked his lies. He made a public spectacle of his rebellion and evil and revealed what the enemy is truly capable of. He showed that evil is real.

Jesus also disarmed the visible human powers of this world. The Jewish religious system was proud of its morality, yet Jesus preached a higher moral standard then the religious system (and lived it). The Roman political system was proud of its unified and just Pax Romana, yet Jesus established a community with a deeper unity and justice than the Roman empire. And in his death he unmasked and disarmed these systems. At the cross the religious leaders denied God as their King and killed the Messiah they had long waited for; at the cross the "perfect" Roman justice system condemned an innocent man in a court case flawed by corruption. At the cross these revered human systems were exposed as insufficient and ultimately enemies of God.

But the main focus in Colossians is our fallen nature. Just like the visible and invisible powers of this world, the human heart is trying to be God, trying to be self-sufficient. Yet we are not self-sufficient, and in our selfishness we hurt one another. We cheat and lie; we destroy marriages and families; we cause war, death, and injustice. It all happens inside of us. We need to perceive who we really are. We are selfish. The way we treat people, what we say on Facebook, what we say to our husband or wife, what we do when no one is looking is proof of that.

How do we deal with it? We ignore it; we try to forget. Or we blame someone or something else. But the cross brings a different solution, a subversive solution: forgiveness. Jesus cannot ignore sin, and rather than blame someone else, he takes our blame upon himself.

It doesn't work to try to forget or ignore things that we have done. We need forgiveness. And only one person can give us that—the one who is above all principalities and powers, above the world's systems and the Devil. Jesus offers complete forgiveness. And that is sufficient to subvert my own heart and bring complete regeneration—a chance to start again.

The cross is the power of God. It begins in my heart and goes on to subvert the visible and invisible powers, transforming the world, society and spiritual reality around me. Every time the cross is preached, the Devil is exposed as a defeated enemy; the system and authorities are exposed as oppressors; the poor are favoured, the captive are set free, and the human heart is regenerated. This is subversive.

Provocative Truth

Once we've had a fresh revelation of the power, essence, and centrality of the cross, then we will want to proclaim it from the rooftops to our generation. How can we do this in today's global culture? We've already discussed the importance of giving people the opportunity to experience God's power and encounter Jesus. Here I want to emphasise the importance of knowing how to ask good questions and creatively communicate the truth.

One of my favourite street artists is the infamous and yet somehow anonymous Banksy, from the UK. What intrigues me is his creative way of asking powerful questions that make you stop and think deeply about things that we often just accept as normal.

Amidst the rouble of a demolished building he painted a small boy with a wet paintbrush standing next to the words "I remember when all this was trees". Simple, subtle, and at the same time a slap in the face. It's like he's asking, "Why the heck did we knock down all those trees and build this big building, to then demolish it and leave this mess in its place?"

Another one I like is a series of Che Guevara images gradually fading across a bridge in London. During the day, under this bridge, a market sells cheap clothes, including one of those great rock T-shirt stalls that always has the famous Che Guevara T-shirt with that same well-known iconic image. The way the series of identical images cleverly fades and distorts across the bridge is subtly asking, "Haven't we worn out the image? Has the revolution just become a fashion?"

Art is powerful. It says what words alone cannot say. It reveals the depth of the human soul, as the artist shares his heart, mind, and worldview. It is a form of communication that is at the same time subtle and provocative. Art shouts out loud; it challenges the status quo and defies convention. It asks powerful questions. Questions can bring about change.

Francis Schaeffer believed in the power of questions. As an apologist he would ask people questions about their worldview—what they believed, and how they explained reality. He would show that at some point our human assumptions about reality fail us and leave us incomplete, showing our desperate need for God. Through questions, Schaeffer would provoke people to re-think, at the deepest level, the basis of their belief system and awareness of reality.

> Every man is somewhere along the line between the real world and the logical conclusions of his non-Christian presuppositions... When we have discovered, as well as we can, a person's point of tension, the next step is to push him toward the logical conclusion of his presuppositions... This is what shows him his need. The Scriptures then show him the nature of his lostness and the answer to it.[1]

I believe this is what Christian art should be doing today. It should be provoking people at the deepest level to re-think assumptions that are accepted by everyone as reality. Christian art should be challenging the predominant worldview that declares humankind to be at the centre and Jesus to be a small detail in the box called religion. Christian art should be asking powerful and revolutionary questions and pointing people to Jesus, the author of reality. And yet it is rare to find art that does this. Have we made our message a worn-out icon? Maybe Banksy's message at the bridge in London is for us. Has our revolution just become a trend?

First of all, we will never truly be vessels of such a provocative art movement if the truth hasn't really hit us. It will not happen until we first meet the holy, almighty, and overwhelmingly powerful creator of the universe and surrender all to him. Once I can say with Paul that "But whatever were gains to me I now consider loss for the sake of Christ" (Phil. 3:7), then I can "become all things to all people" (1 Cor. 9:22) and be an artist that truly engages with the scene.

Then we will come to realise that following a fashion trend is easy, but being at the cutting edge of a truly provocative Christian art movement will take hard work. It means hours of prayer. It means really understanding the world around us and knowing the people our art connects with. It takes deep thought and reflection. It takes work to refine and perfect our art to a level that really touches the heart and soul. It will require incredible boldness, sharp creativity, and thinking outside the box to ask the right questions.

As we went around clubs playing with Alegorica and sharing the good news about Jesus, our concerts often ended with hours of deep conversations with people. Some great questions would come up in these conversations, and we were learning more about the way people thought and the issues they had with faith and Christianity. These questions and conversations gave us inspiration for lyrics and new parts for our show as we sought to engage with the themes that were in the hearts and minds of our audience.

Some would say things like "that's cool you believe in Jesus. I'm still thinking about what I believe, but I think all ways lead to God. So it doesn't really matter". So we wrote a song called "Spirituality", in which I would dress up like a priest and the lyrics were a mix of words and terminology from different religions and ideologies, and in the chorus we would sing, "If you don't know where you're going, any road will do".

Others we talked to seemed more concerned about money, careers, and just enjoying life. So we wrote a song called "Plastic gods", in which our actress dressed up like Lady Gaga and the band would bow down to a shop mannequin while African drum beats created a weird ritualistic tribal worship vibe.

My favourite kind of lyrics were ones that protested, in a kind of punk fashion, against the predominant secular humanist mindset. I love that, because most people think along the lines of secular humanism without realising it, and they think protests should be against politics or religion. So we turn the tables and question the self-centred false hope of humanism, with lyrics like "In this world order, who is more important than us, our rights, and our ambitions? We don't need religious figures anymore, just someone to take out our rubbish". The irony of it can make people stop and think: "wait a minute, that doesn't sound right".

Art is a powerful language and through it we can ask important questions, but speaking truth into the music and art scene today can be intimidating. The gospel is so countercultural. Possibly one of the more intimidating obstacles is the underlying belief that faith should be a private matter and not to be spoken of in public. Based on this assumption people will say that we shouldn't "use" the platform of art and music to preach. Or that art with a message is propaganda.

I disagree on two levels. First, I believe people want to discuss and hear about life, God, morality, spirituality, and the like because deep down they are hungry for truth. Second, I believe that when I create, my art is essentially an expression of myself—my talent, ideas, questions, beliefs, and often the deepest things that words can't express. Therefore, if my faith is at the centre of my life, it will come out in my art. My art will always have a message, the message that is closest to my heart.

People are thirsty to talk about topics that matter, the big questions, the God questions. So don't be afraid to speak the truth in your art and the scene God has called you to.

Clear Truth

The gospel is powerful, subversive, provocative, but what exactly is the gospel? This has already been laid out mostly through this chapter, but I don't want to end without being as clear and simple as possible about what I mean when I say "speak the truth".

To get clear on what the message of the gospel actually is, the best way, of course, is to look at the Bible. Let's start with the good news that Jesus preached: "After John was put in prison, Jesus went into Galilee, proclaiming the good news of God. 'The time has come,' he said. 'The kingdom of God has come near. Repent and believe the good news!' (Mark 1:14-15).

Jesus started his ministry by going everywhere and proclaiming that the kingdom of God is near, that the year of the Lord has come. In Luke 4 we see Jesus reading from the scroll of Isaiah, the prophesy about the year of the Lord, the day the captives would be set free, the blind would see. He hands back the scroll and declares: "Today this scripture is fulfilled in your hearing" (Luke 4:21). Jesus made it more than clear everywhere he went that he was bringing the kingdom of God, that he was the year of the Lord, that he was what everyone had been waiting for.

Throughout the Gospel of John, we read how Jesus pointed to himself as the salvation all were waiting for. –He said:

> "Whoever drinks the water I give them will never thirst". (John 4:14)

> "I am the bread of life". (John 6:35)

> "I am the good shepherd". (John 10:11)

> "I have come into the world as a light, so that no one who believes in me should stay in darkness". (John 12:46)

> "I am the way and the truth and the life". (John 14:6)

Often people have tried to make the gospel into a system, a series of principals or truths that you have to tell someone, and once they accept each step they are saved. When I read the gospel I understand that really it's a story about a person: Jesus. The gospel is Jesus. We need to present Jesus to people. But what do we say about him?

Reading through the book of Acts is really insightful because in it we observe what message the disciples preached after Jesus went back to the Father. The very first evangelistic message preached by the apostles after the Holy Spirit came down on them was Peter addressing a Jewish audience in Jerusalem (Acts 2). Using the Jewish Bible (the Old Testament) as his basis, Peter showed that Jesus is the Messiah and explained how he died and rose again. In Acts 10, we read how Peter preached the gospel for the first time to a non-Jewish audience. Rather than turning to the Jewish Scriptures, he started by saying that God accepts every nation, and then he went on to explain again how Jesus died and rose again. In Acts 17, Paul preached to a group of Greek philosophers in Athens. He started by commenting on their religiosity and desire to seek and know God, observing their many idols and statues. He also quoted one of their poets. As he pointed to God, the Creator, he turned to Jesus, God's appointed man, whom he raised from the dead.

When the apostles preached, they basically spoke about Jesus. They addressed each audience according to their situation and context. They went to people and spoke in a way they could understand, but the core of the message was always the same: Jesus is the Son of God (divine); he rose from the dead; and all must repent, believe in him, and be baptised.

In his letter to the Corinthians Paul described the core of his message: "For what I received I passed on to you as of first importance: that Christ died for our sins according to the Scriptures, that he was buried, that he was raised on the third day according to the Scriptures" (1 Cor. 15:3-4).

Too often we forget the importance of keeping this message simple and clear. It seems easier to share a nice story about our lives, share our testimony, or tell people that God loves them. This may be a good start, but it's not the gospel. The gospel is Jesus and the truth about his death and resurrection. Dietrich Bonhoeffer, the German theologian who stood against the Nazi power during the Second World War, called us back to the essentials: "Does not our preaching contain too much of our own opinion and convictions, and too little of Jesus Christ?"[2]

Paul wrote to the Philippians when he was under house arrest in Rome. He declared he was in chains because of the message about Jesus. He also shared with the church in Philippi about people out there who were envious of him and trying to discredit him. But he celebrated both his chains and the attacks to his reputation because he said that in every way, "whether from false motives or true, Christ is preached" (Phil. 1:18). Paul can only say this because his message was clear and straight. His emphasis was not himself, what he had done, his story, or his ministry. His focus was always Jesus. And because of this, when he suffered, he suffered for Jesus. Even when envious people tried to compete with him, they preached Jesus!

Sharing Jesus can seem intimidating to many, but I have found that whenever we step out in faith and boldness, each in our own way, seeing God at work in someone's life suddenly puts everything into perspective and reminds us what really matters. It is exciting and invigorating.

Of course, we're all called to do this in different ways. Some are more gifted at sharing Jesus through a close relationship. Others are good at spontaneous one-on-one encounters. Others are called to address small groups in the street. God uses others to address large crowds in clubs or even football stadiums. But whatever way God uses us, whatever opportunities he gives us, our generation needs to hear the truth. And my prayer is that we find the most creative and impactful ways to proclaim the truth to the largest unreached culture today.

In the opportunities God gives you, start by seeking to understand what that person or group of people already knows and believes, what's going on in their lives and what are their questions and barriers to the gospel. Share your own faith in a natural way. Don't feel like you have to blurt it all out on every encounter, but let God lead you and give you opportunities. Share your personal testimony if it makes sense. Look for connections and opportunities to show how the way you see the world is guided by your relationship with Jesus.

But ultimately look for that right moment to explain who Jesus is, his divinity, his love, death, and resurrection. Talk about why we need him, about our human nature, our fallen hearts, and our sin. When that person or group is ready, call them to repentance, explain how we need God's forgiveness, and let them know what it means to surrender all to Jesus as we choose to follow him.

You may not get a chance to say everything you want, but the most important thing is that people get a chance to meet Jesus personally. Offer prayer, as this is a good way for people to become aware of his presence. Pray that they might know him and that he would reveal himself to them.

Speak the truth.

9

Stay Together

In São Paulo, if we had simply gone into the scene, preached a message, and then told people to go to church, most wouldn't have made it. The cultural gap between the church and our global culture presents a huge challenge for many. In fact, that's one of the most common questions we get when we share about our evangelistic projects: "What do you do with people when they respond? What's next?" We know how hard it can be, especially for a young person, to just walk into a church. After we share the message we need to stay together.

Learning to follow Jesus needs to start in the scene, in the context people come from. This is becoming all things to all men. Not only did Paul go to the Greeks to preach Jesus, but he spent time with them, often years. He lived among them and showed them what it meant to be a Greek who followed Jesus. This is discipleship, that age old practise of learning to follow Jesus and helping others to do the same. There's nothing new here. But we need to think about the context we're in today and address some of the specific challenges for someone living in this global culture to learn to follow Jesus.

I think the first and most important thing is that people get the chance to meet bold and genuine followers of Jesus who are alive in their faith, filled with the Holy Spirit, in love with the Word, part of a welcoming community and actively demonstrating what it means to follow Jesus today.

Just as our current relativistic culture presents challenges in sharing Jesus, it also offers difficulties in making disciples for Jesus. Making a decision to follow Jesus doesn't make everything clear instantly. Until a new believer is grounded in the Word of God, they may be confused about what to believe and how to define truth. For that reason, one of the most important things in discipleship today is making the Bible accessible to people where they are. That means good solid Bible study and teaching in a language and format that is accessible to the Global Youth Culture. This is a huge challenge for a generation that is constantly on the move, with no time for commitment and depth. But once they discover the awesome Word of God and experience its power, they will be infected with a hunger for its life-giving and coherent truth.

Consumerism has led to loss of identity and superficial relationships. It has also led to a loss of passion. People don't have anything to fight for anymore. I believe the key response to these specific challenges lies in an alive and actively engaged community of Jesus followers. Building a Holy Spirit filled, united, and welcoming community can revert the chain of lies behind this socially fragmented and detached culture.

When we strip away the unnecessary "church culture" and live as the community of believers Jesus intended us to be, the church is a miracle, unique and unprecedented in society today. The church should be a community of all ages, all social backgrounds, all ethnic groups, and all walks of life, united by one truth, one spirit and one baptism, living out a love based on grace and forgiveness. Society does not and cannot offer anything like this, and yet this is what we all are looking for. It is there that we can experience acceptance for who we are and rediscover a genuine identity. And given the chance to get involved in the action of this powerful gospel movement, we also discover again the passion of being an agent of change in society. Involvement in social transformation, sharing the good news and making disciples is the best remedy for the numbness that comes from living in a consumerist society.

When we grasp this vision of the church, our biggest and most important task is to build bridges. We need to find a way of welcoming people into this community and dispelling their prejudices and negative picture of the church. Without a doubt there is also the need for renewal and revival inside the church, but here I want to focus on that front line and the bridge to the church. With that mission in mind, we have sought to identify as partners strong and healthy churches that are dynamic, open, and welcoming to young people.

Discipleship is a life-long process that begins before we even choose to follow Jesus. As God draws near to us throughout our lives, constantly calling us home, there are key moments of insight and learning through which we become more and more aware of His awesome reality. These are the beginnings of discipleship. And as we come in contact with the gospel message spoken and lived out by Christian witnesses, we start to learn and understand more about Jesus' love, grace, and forgiveness. Ultimately, we learn that he is Lord, and we need to surrender to him.

When we understand this process, we realise that discipleship must start wherever people are. As we go to them with the good news, we are already in that awesome process of making disciples. Often, we put discipleship into a box. When we think of discipleship, we think of things like a Bible class at church or a formal one-on-one mentoring relationship. These are important things to do, but discipleship doesn't start the day a young person walks into church. Church culture can be intimidating to a new believer. We tend to expect them to be at church the next Sunday wearing the appropriate clothes and saying the right things. We then tell them they need to be "ministered to" and need to sit and listen to sermons for the next three years before they might be allowed to play guitar in worship. The poor dude sits there thinking, "but I don't even like playing that kind of music".

Discipleship needs to happen in the context where people come from. As we go to people and share the good news in a relevant way where they are, we need to give people the opportunity to start understanding and growing in their faith where they are too. When this happens, we will see fruit. A young believer learning to follow Jesus in the scene he comes from, learning to be salt and light to that world, with his friends and network of contacts, has a powerful effect. He becomes a missionary from day one as he continues to be engaged in his own environment and relationships, leading others to faith.

These disciples are the most effective and influential in reaching the global culture. They become agents of change and trend setters in a globalised society, front-liners in the spreading of the kingdom in a fast and changing world. 'The response of the disciple is an act of obedience, not a confession of faith in Jesus.'[1]

But first let's go to the source to remember what discipleship is all about.

Jesus the Disciple Maker

Brazilian author Augusto Cury is a physician and psychiatrist who studied the functioning of the mind. He has become one of the most popular authors in Brazil. His first novel, *O Futuro da Humanidade* (The Future of Humanity), tells the story of a man who becomes homeless in an attempt to isolate himself from society. The main character, a medical student who befriends the homeless man, challenges this concept by explaining that it is impossible to be truly isolated from the world around us:

> No one is a physical, psychological or social island in humanity. We are all influenced by others. All our acts, whether conscious or unconscious, being constructive or destructive attitudes, alter events and the development of humanity itself.[2]

Whether we intend to or not, we are influencing people around us. You might be a positive or a negative influence, and this might be purposeful, or you might be completely unaware of it. On one hand this brings a weight of responsibility. On the other hand, this is a huge opportunity. We have the chance to truly make a difference to the world around us if we are purposeful in our words and actions.

Jesus was very purposeful as he taught and influenced those around him. In fact, it was his key strategy. He called men to walk with him, and he taught them to be like him. These, in turn, taught others to be like Jesus. This is discipleship. ·.

As result, for the early church, being a Christian meant being a disciple and making disciples. It meant applying your mind and life to being like Jesus in attitude and actions, and it meant fulfilling the great commission to go and make disciples of all the nations (Matt. 28:19).

Jesus used two main methods of teaching: being and sending. "He appointed twelve that they might be with him and that he might send them out to preach" (Mark 3:14).

The beginning of this relationship between Jesus and his disciples is quite remarkable. He walks up to a few fishermen and simply says "Follow me, and I will send you out to fish for people" (Mark1:17). Something about Jesus' authority and manner drew these men to him, and his first request is that they walk with him. "Follow me", he said. Spending time together was a crucial part of Jesus' discipleship lifestyle.

As Jesus spent time with his disciples, sometimes he would teach. "When he was alone with his own disciples, he explained everything". (Mark 4:34) Other times he called them to rest. "Come with me by yourselves to a quiet place and get some rest" (Mark 6:31). Even the most common everyday situations became opportunities for learning, like when Jesus uses an argument between the disciples on the road to teach humility (Mark 9:33-35).

But Jesus didn't only teach theory, he sent the disciples out to practise. In Mark 6:7-11 we see Jesus sending the disciples out to preach, cast out demons, and heal the sick. Later when the disciples come to Jesus to tell him that his audience was hungry and needed food, Jesus responds with something like "you do something about it!" (Mark 6:37)

Jesus makes discipleship a lifestyle, a simple day-to-day relationship. He used everyday situations to teach and give people a chance to get involved in the action. This is still the most effective way of making disciples today, especially in the context of the Global Youth Culture. In a world of scepticism and antagonism toward institutions and programs, we need a genuine and natural approach to making disciples. A generation with broken relationships and in identity crisis, is thirsty for someone to give of themselves, for deep relational learning. A generation that has lost its purpose and passion can be awakened by the chance to get involved by the challenge to "do something about it!"

Barnabas the Disciple Maker

I expect most readers have heard of Paul, the apostle. But how much do you know about Barnabas? Barnabas was a disciple maker, and a close read of Acts shows Barnabas' gift was key to Paul's first steps as a believer.

We first hear of Barnabas in Acts 4, where he is nicknamed the encourager. The relationship between Barnabas and Paul starts in chapter 9. Paul had met Jesus on the road to Damascus and was changed, but everyone was afraid to meet him, even the apostles. Barnabas came along and encouraged Paul to meet the apostles, presenting him to them, using his credibility to give Paul a chance.

In chapter 11, Barnabas is given a really important task by the apostles. For the first time, some non-Jewish believers were forming a church in Antioch, and the apostles sent Barnabas to check out what's happening there. At that point, Paul was back in his home town, apparently not doing much, waiting for an opportunity. Barnabas called Paul to get involved and takes him to Antioch.

By chapter 12 of Acts, Barnabas and Paul had formed such a friendship and partnership that the church of Antioch decided to send them out as a missionary team. During that trip, on mission to Lystra

(Acts 14), the Greeks decided they must be gods because they heal a lame man. They called Barnabas Zeus (the main god) and Paul Hermes, "because he was the chief speaker" (Acts 14:12). Barnabas still seemed to be the leader but was having Paul do all the speaking. So again, we see Barnabas encouraging Paul, lifting him up, spurring him on in his gifting.

Acts 15 tells us about this curious situation where the two close friends fight and came to such irreconcilable differences they chose to part ways. Barnabas wanted to bring Mark on one of their trips, but Paul didn't want him there. Mark had given up and left the team on a previous trip, and for Paul, Mark was not suitable for service. Barnabas the encourager wanted to give Mark another chance. While it's hard to understand how such godly men could not work this out, the fact was Paul went on to plant churches everywhere and write a big part of the New Testament, while Barnabas invested his time in Mark, who went on to serve both Peter and Paul at different times in the future. In fact, it's quite likely that was the same Mark who wrote the gospel by the same name.

Barnabas invested his life in other people. He wasn't in the spotlight much, but because of him, we have Paul, Mark, and a majority of the New Testament. Barnabas knew of the exponential power in disciple making.

Bible

Studying the Bible with the hardcore guys in Guarulhos, many of whom had never read the Bible before, was amazing. Often someone reading a passage for the first time brings the best comments and insights, as they have a fresh perspective and a curiosity we sadly seem to lose with years of being "in the church". One time after we finished reading Jesus' parable of the lost son, I looked up and Rafael, a tall dude with full arm tattoo sleeves, was in tears. "Rafael, are you ok?" I asked.

"It's such a beautiful story", he said.

"But surely you've heard this before? Everyone knows this story".

"No, I've never heard it", he explained, "It's so cool how the father was waiting for the son to come home".

"Yes" I said, "Jesus told this story so we might understand how God feels about us".

We wanted these new believers to feel part of a community, to be part of the church, but it was a big step. Studying the Bible together, first in their own context, meant they had the chance to understand more about Jesus and what it meant to follow him. Reading until the end of the gospel story, we got to the part where Jesus sends the disciples to baptise people and make more followers. I asked if they wanted to get baptised, and seven of them said yes.

Now, I come from a traditional Baptist church in England and Baptists always have cool baptistries under the stage at church. So I asked Sandro, our pastor, if I could put a bathtub in Projeto 242 for baptisms. There's something really special about a baptism in church with everyone gathered around in worship. It's more intimate than going to some swimming pool somewhere. So I bought an old cast-iron bathtub, renovated it, and prepared a cool space in the church for the baptism.

For some of these guys, the first time they were coming to a church service was to get baptised. It was a powerful moment, and we were all really impacted by God's awesome presence. One guy from the church made a video that he uploaded to YouTube, and not long after that we had others contacting us asking if they could get baptised in our bathtub.

I learned a lot with these guys and the whole process. Two aspects of discipleship that I stated earlier in this chapter stand out to me: discipleship needs to start where people are, in their own context, and people need to come in contact with the powerful Word of God.

The hardcore band from Guarulhos needed to learn what it meant for a hardcore band from Guarulhos to follow Jesus, just as the Greeks needed to learn from Paul what it looked like to be a Greek who follows Jesus. Being a Greek who followed Jesus looked different than a Jew who followed Jesus. It presented different challenges and opportunities. If I had just told the guys to go to church, I may not have seen much of them after that. Going to them, spending time with them in their rehearsal, hanging out at shows and in their homes, was essential for me to understand who they were and where they were coming from. And it was essential for them to see more closely what life with Jesus could look like.

We also need to realise the powerful result of making the Word of God accessible to people where they are. The first time I figured this out was when I was in high school. My dad worked with the Christian student movement in universities in Brazil. A big part of what he did was giving students access to the Bible in a setting that was welcoming to them as non-believers. The Bible studies were open discussions where people could explore, debate, and discover who Jesus is for themselves. So I decided I wanted to try this out in my high school.

I invited some friends to join me in running a Bible discussion group during our school break. They were unbelievers, but had a Catholic upbringing, and they were curious. We got permission to use a classroom and had a group of twenty or so join us for the first few months. But then the school director called me to her office one day and told me I had to end the Bible study group because it could cause "religious conflict" in the school. This made me an angry teenager.

I went home, dressed in black, and hung a sign on my shoulders that read "God is dead" on the front and "…for many people" on the back. I went to school dressed like that and marched around in protest during the break time. People kept asking what was wrong and why I was dressed like that. I explained that we had been prohibited from having a Bible study at school. Soon a whole bunch of people who had never been to a Bible study were joining in! "Yeah! We want the right to have a Bible study in our school!" We got a petition going to get the Bible study back; hundreds of students signed it.

We never really got a response from the director, but we decided that was enough for us to just keep on with the Bible study. Our group doubled in size and gained a new momentum. As we went through the gospel people would come prepared with questions and challenges, curiously discovering a text they'd always heard about but never really read.

As I shared at the beginning of the book, I found a similar result in discussing the Bible with young people in our café project in London and in our Bible study in Guarulhos. When we allow people the chance to read the Word, ask questions, and discuss it in their own environment and in a language they understand, we discover they have a deep hunger for truth.

The main emphasis of an informal Bible study (see page 165 for a guide) is helping people who have possibly never read the Bible, or even walked into a church, find community and contact with the Word of God and meet God as He powerfully reveals Himself through the stories and lessons of Scripture. It's important to avoid it becoming another meeting for Christians. Instead it should be a place where people of all different backgrounds and beliefs can feel welcome, ask questions, say things you don't usually say in a church, disagree, and discuss relevant topics. With that in mind, it's clear that trying to run an informal Bible study without first really engaging with the scene as described in the previous chapters, doesn't really work.

An informal Bible study should happen in a venue that is comfortable, familiar, and easily accessible for the audience described above. It might be a café, a club, a cultural centre, a community house, or another place where people naturally gather.

Most Bible studies or discipleship courses in church are very structured and follow a lesson or lecture format. One person in the front explains what the Bible is saying and teaches people what the principles are and how they should apply them in their lives. For people who have never been to church, these meetings can seem like going back to school. They are too formal and often involve words and terms they don't understand.

Informal Bible studies are about reading the Bible for ourselves, discovering its message and the living God behind it. We do this by focusing on the passages rather than a teacher and asking good questions as a group to discover what the passage is saying. Young people today are sceptical of institutions and authority and are not inclined to just sit and listen to a leader explain what they should believe. For a generation that is used to finding their own answers and making their own decisions, the concept of discovering the answers for themselves really resonates.

In this mission movement God has called us to, one of my prayers is that Bible study would be a central part of our culture as we reach global youth. I pray for dynamic teams in every city that will be relevantly engaging the youth culture and meeting around the Bible, letting the inherent power of the Word of God change our hearts and minds.

Community

The Global Youth Culture faces a crisis of relationship. And genuine community around the Word is the answer. A community centred on the gospel is often someone's first encounter with authentic relationships. The sense of purpose and acceptance in community makes it easier to discovery one's identity in Jesus.

Dietrich Bonhoeffer considered community to be the greatest privilege of the Christian. The community he praised was not the common pattern of meeting once a week, but a day-to-day shared life worshipping, reading the Word, praying, eating, and working together.[3]

Lindsay Olesberg is the Scripture manager for the Urbana Student Missions Convention. She has overseen Bible study and exegesis at major evangelical gatherings throughout the world. She talks about the importance of community in the context of studying the Bible:

When we gather together, with the Scripture at the center of our communal life, something beautiful develops. Studying the Bible in community grounds us, feeds us, weaves us together and launches us out into the world to take our part in God's mission.[4]

The barriers of a cultural gap between the church and the outside world and the unfamiliarity that a newcomer faces when walking into a church service hinders real community. For authentic community to happen, we need the church people, not the church building and program. In that sense community can and should be available to not-yet-believers *before* they come to a Sunday service. This can happen anywhere in our normal day-to-day lives—a Bible study in a cafe, at a party, at a festival, or in a gathering in our homes.

All it takes is for the church to purposefully create and nurture environments that encourage genuine community, where new people feel welcome. This means we need to seek out opportunities to spend time together with people who are not part of our closed circle of Christians. A life open and shared with others as you welcome people into your life, your home, and your walk with Jesus can lead to deeper relationships than you can form in a weekly meeting.

Life in community must then lead to action. Bonhoeffer explained that community gives the person the opportunity to put their faith into practice by sharing it with others. Getting people practically involved in the kingdom plays a powerful role in discipleship. When we find acceptance, truth, and identity, we also find the passion to be involved in changing the World around us.

After their baptism, the Guarulhos team continued meeting weekly to study the Bible together. As I mentioned earlier, they immediately started sharing their faith more and more with friends and through their band. I told them they were already missionaries and invited them to the Steiger Mission School in Germany (SMS).

Alex, Robson, Moah, and Felipe came to the SMS in Germany in 2012. Some of them were starting a new band. All of them were involved in the scene and wanted to know more about what they could do for Jesus. The following year, Moah got married, and his wife, Flavia, who had also been a key part of the Bible study, came to the SMS. Ficko, an influential graffiti artist from São Paulo, who had been part of the Bible study, also attended the SMS that year.

At the SMS they heard about a concept we've practised in different places around the world with our Steiger teams: community houses. Basically a few of our Steiger team in a city choose to live together and open their home to others. This creates a centre for the action of the mission, a meeting place for friends and people interested in the message. We often host open mic nights, parties, and small concerts in the home. People who are interested in learning to follow Jesus can also move in and be part of the community. This is discipleship seven days a week in an informal and relational way as the team lives together, shares the bills, eats meals together, prays together, and studies the Bible together.

Alex, Moah, and Flavia suggested we could start a community house in Guarulhos, where they were all from. So Ania and I, with our son, Daniel, who was three at the time, decided to move in with the team. We rented a house in Guarulhos that was large enough for around eight people to live, plus a separate little house in the backyard, which was ideal for our small family. This started an amazing period of two years together, learning to follow Jesus in day-to-day life, hanging out, talking, praying, studying the Word, and having lots of parties and events. The house was always packed. We had events once a month for bands, artists, and friends, most of whom had never been to a church. A lot of people got to know Jesus this way.

I have to admit, it was challenging at times. Living in close community always is, as we all have bad days. It's easy to be nice to someone you only see once a week on Sunday. But being together in and out every day—through bad moods in the mornings, when tired after a long day at work, when going through a crisis—means people see you at your worst. These are all great opportunities to learn real love and forgiveness.

In addition to the original Bible study group, many others joined the Bible studies, became regular visitors, and participated in the events. Our events often drew one hundred or more people, packing out the back garden and living room. Eventually we had new people moving in and becoming part of the community.

A guy people called "Xarope" would hang out with us often on Saturdays. He was a "straight edge" vegan, a movement connected to the hardcore scene. Adherents stick to pretty strict rules and standards related to diet and ideology. He had a tattoo of a church in flames on his neck, so clearly he was not into religion very much. One day he asked if he could move in with us. "I feel more at home here than in my own home. You guys seem to care about me more than my family does".

I had reservations and probed: "You know we pray and read the Bible here right? You want to be part of something like that?"

Xarope answered confidently, "Yes, I want to learn about Jesus. I think it will do me some good".

He lived with us for about six months; it was a really interesting time. He participated in all the Bible studies and prayer times, and we became good friends. He came from a troubled background and didn't find it easy to maintain good relationships. One day he just decided to leave. After a while, he got back in touch, telling us that the time he spent in the house was one of the most important times in his life. He asked us to pray for him, as he was going through some hard times.

Another great guy who joined our community was Cascata, an old friend of Moah's and Xarope's. The first day he visited he brought a crate of beer and discussed politics all afternoon. He was a street artist and political activist who had also spent time traveling around Brazil on a bicycle selling hippie jewellery and paintings. He was known for having painted a figure of a kind of new age cartoon cow character all over town. He asked to move in and frequented our prayer times and Bible studies. He wouldn't say much, but he seemed open to what we were studying and sharing.

One Sunday morning, as we were walking out to go to church, Cascata came out with his skateboard.

"Where are you off to?" I asked.

"Church", he said.

"Really? You're coming with us?" I asked, surprised.

"No, I'm going to my church", he answered proudly.

"What? You go to church? What church? And since when?"

He then explained that he had started going to a small local church some weeks before. It was amazing, and kind of amusing, to see this subtle yet deep change in Cascata. He just decided to start going to a church without telling us. He didn't ask to go to the church we went to. He just decided to find his own!

At the end of 2015, when Ania and I felt called to return to Europe and serve with Steiger there, we were able to pass the leadership of the community house over to Moah and Flavia. It was amazing to see how much God had grown both of them over time and how passionate they were about serving Jesus and reaching people.

While it was hard for us to leave all our friends in Brazil and the amazing ministry God had allowed us to be part of in São Paulo, at the same time it was deeply satisfying to see that work continue with some of the young guys and girls we'd spent so much time with. The band Alegorica continued under the leadership of a young guy named Bruno. He joined as a bass player years before and went to the SMS in 2014. Moah kept the Manifeste events going, as well as the community house together with Flavia. Angelo and Aline, who had been part of the Manifeste team, went on to become admin and communication leaders for Steiger Brazil. Many others shared the load, and the team keeps growing.

10

Join the Revolution

R oughly the last twelve years have been about developing Steiger from a movement to a mission organisation. We've worked on this because we believe God has called us to have a meaningful impact on our generation today. Most of the time, it seems we're just trying to keep up with what we see God doing.

Today, Steiger has teams in the USA, Brazil, Chile, Colombia, Germany, Switzerland, Poland, Finland, Ukraine, Belarus, New Zealand, and Lebanon, and new teams starting in Portugal, Russia, Kazakhstan, and more—all with awesome, dedicated people. Our vision is to radically and eternally change the world by raising up missionaries who will present Jesus to the Global Youth Culture. And we are realizing this vision as God is drawing young people to himself. His heart is broken for this generation and He is on the move. He is revealing Himself through this new wave of missionary teams who boldly and relevantly preach the gospel, dedicate themselves to finding truth in Scripture, pray for healing and salvation on the streets and clubs, and courageously build long-term relationships and communities in city centres around the world.

At the beginning of 2018, as I prayed about where God was leading us as a mission in Europe, I felt led to pray for different cities around the continent. I looked over a list of the most populated and influential European cities and felt God challenging me to pray for Steiger teams to start up in all of those cities. I thought about how amazing it would be to have powerful and dynamic missionary teams dedicated to reaching the Global Youth Culture in one hundred cities in Europe. It could bring a real impact for the gospel in Europe and the world.

Later that year I wrote the vision down, describing a model of what we now call a Steiger City Team. This also became the international vision for Steiger, to establish one hundred Steiger City Teams by 2025. A Steiger City Team is a dynamic, multi-gifted, and multi-denominational missionary team (including full-time missionary leaders and volunteers), specialised in reaching the Global Youth Culture of a key urban centre. Because a Steiger team both unifies and mobilises the church, it is a small yet powerful catalyst for God to impact an entire city. We accomplish this through long-term, ongoing, and relevant evangelism and discipleship and strategic local church partnership.

For instance, our team in Kiev, has gathered more than seventy people from various churches to go to the streets, shopping malls, and youth hostels every week to share Jesus with young Ukrainians. Our team in Wroclaw, Poland, runs two evangelistic café and art centres in partnership with four local churches, reaching and discipling young people in the city every week. Some of the team members run a community house similar to the one I described from Guarulhos, São Paulo. Our team in Beirut, Lebanon, makes short films creatively introducing Christianity that are screened in universities, leading to deep discussions with the students. They have developed a great relationship with the atheist student club and the Muslim student club. Sometimes they go for picnics together in the mountains.

In addition to our local teams, Steiger has various international catalytic tools, like Come&Live! – a platform to encourage bands and artists to share the gospel in a secular context. Bands like Nuteki from Minsk, Belarus, regularly tour all over the Russian-speaking world playing concerts to thousands of young people. They boldly preach Jesus in every show and plant Bible studies in cafés along the way.

No Longer Music continues touring around the world. In Europe we have a festival-size mobile stage trailer, which is great for the large production and mainstream music style now characteristic of NLM. With this tool we have been able to roll up to main squares all over Europe and lift up a powerful depiction of the cross, complete with special effects, in a very public and clear way to thousands of people. It's like Billy Graham rock 'n' roll style!

Come&Live! is also producing weekly blogs and podcasts inspiring thousands of young bands and artists to use their God-given talents to share Jesus in the scene. We have also partnered with artists like Brian "Head" Welch, from the band Korn, providing him with missionary teams at concerts to share Jesus with Korn fans. Brian met Jesus years ago, and after a time away from the band, he felt called to go back to Korn and share his story with people around the world. Over the last two years, working with Brian to reach fans at Korn concerts even led us to Japan where Steiger's director, Aaron Pierce, has started pioneering new opportunities for Steiger in that part of the world.

Fingerprint is another movement under Steiger. In 2008 Stephan and Nadine Maag, passionate followers of Jesus, started a street-evangelism ministry in Switzerland. They joined Steiger in 2018. It has spread like a wild fire, encouraging all our Steiger teams around the world to go to the streets with flash mobs, creative interactions, or just to simply offer prayer or stand on a chair and proclaim the good news. This happens even in countries where it is illegal to preach the gospel publicly, and yet our bold missionary teams have not let that stop them. Recently our Kiev team was involved in an important youth conference called Holy Spirit Night (which started in Germany). The team led four hundred conference participants to boldly share their faith on the streets of the city and bring over one thousand visitors to the conference the following day! Fingerprint teams were all around Moscow and St Petersburg during the world cup of 2018. At the conclusion of their outreach, they had talked personally with 904 people, prayed for 362 people, and saw 53 people surrender their lives to Jesus.

We have also developed tools to support our teams in the important work of discipleship and church partnering. IsThereMore is a discipleship tool that includes articles, videos, and an informal Bible study online. Our #Engage project trains our teams to form strong and long-term partnerships with local churches to help them reach young people in their cities.

I believe this is only the beginning. Maybe God is calling you to be part of this vision! I want to end by sharing clearly what Steiger's values are and how you can get involved.

Steiger's Values

At Steiger we've found it to be crucially important to stay strong in a few key values as we seek to obey God's calling on our lives. Especially as we do things outside the box, we want to reach the scene and not be reached by it. So it is vitally important for us to stay close to God personally and remain Bible-based and Gospel-centred in our message. This is what keeps this movement growing strong. These are our values:

Seek God: God rewards those who seek Him with a desperate heart (Heb, 11:6). The foundation of everything we do stems from a personal relationship with God through Jesus Christ. We acknowledge that God is the source of all authority, power, and opportunities and that apart from the work of the Holy Spirit, all our ministry efforts will be futile (John 15:5). Therefore, passionately seeking God through diligent prayer, in-depth study of the Bible, and heartfelt praise and worship is our first priority.

Cross: "For I resolved to know nothing while I was with you except Jesus Christ and him crucified" (1 Cor. 2:2). We aim to demonstrate the power of God by lifting up the cross outside of the church. The very core and power of the gospel is the death and resurrection of Jesus.

Relevance: "I have become all things to all people so that by all possible means I might save some" (1 Corinthians 9:22). We aim to relevantly (in terms of music, technology, language, and symbols) communicate the message of the Cross in a language that the Global Youth Culture can understand—as modelled by Christ's example and teaching—while at the same time never changing, obscuring, or omitting the gospel message.

Holiness: "In a large house there are articles not only of gold and silver, but also of wood and clay; some are for special purposes and some for common use. Those who cleanse themselves from the latter, he will be an instrument for special purposes, made holy, useful to the Master and prepared to do any good work" (2 Timothy 2:20-21). We want to live a holy and pure lifestyle out of a sincere desire to obey and serve God. We take sin seriously, embrace accountability, and hold each other to high standards. We know that being in public ministry means we are an example for others and that God requires a higher standard from us (James 3:1). Therefore, we limit our freedoms for the sake of others.

Courage: "When they saw the courage of Peter and John and realised that they were unschooled, ordinary men, they were astonished, and they took note that these men had been with Jesus" (Acts 4:13). Courage is not the absence of fear but rather a willingness to step through fear. We believe this courage comes from a deep trust in God and His promises developed by diligent study of His Word and daily commitment to seeking Him. As a person learns to trust God and step through fear, they will grow in their faith and their ability to overcome greater challenges in the future. We want to have the courage to defy conventional thinking; ask for extraordinary things of God; speak the truth boldly, even if it is not popular; take great risks; and sacrifice our safety, security, and reputations all for the sake of the gospel.

Get involved

I hope this book has encouraged and inspired you to think of ways you can serve this important cause to share the truth about Jesus with this lost and broken generation. As I shared at the beginning, the Global Youth Culture is the largest unreached people group today. I believe the front line of missions today is to reach young people in this urban, global, and secularised context.

I also hope that you find the principles and concepts I shared useful to apply in your own context, wherever you are. The first place I encourage you to connect is with a local church. If you're not part of one, find one that believes in and teaches the Bible and encourages people to share their faith outside the church. Put into practise the steps I laid out in chapter 7, "Know the Scene", to start reaching out into your local area.

There is lots happening in different places around the world, so I expect, if you look, you will find places where God is moving, and young people are getting the chance to hear about Jesus. I have had the· privilege to see God moving in many ways through different churches and organisations around the world. God is on the move, and many in the church today have seen the need to change and adapt to the new challenges, making the global secular context a priority and recognising the need to not only reach young people, but to make sure we are including young people in leadership and the decision-making process for the future of the church.

I just recently came from a Lausanne think tank meeting in Amsterdam. Eighty leaders from around Europe were planning for the Lausanne 2020 Dynamic Gospel – New Europe event. Lausanne is one of the most important unifying bodies for evangelical Christianity worldwide, and they focused their last large global gathering on the next generations at Lausanne Younger Leaders 2016.

The International Fellowship of Evangelical Students (IFES, or InterVarsity in the USA) has made important efforts to get students involved in sharing their faith in the universities and also, at events like Urbana and an upcoming European version called Revive, to encourage students to get involved in missions. If you're in a university I encourage you to find out if there is a local Christian student movement you can get connected to.

There are also exciting new church movements led by groups like Hillsong, Bethel, and ICF (in Europe) that are seeking fresh church expressions, powerful worship, bold faith, and making efforts to communicate in a language young people can understand today. Bethel, for instance, has gotten behind an important event called The Send. Run by a collaboration between various ministries like Youth with a Mission, Lifestyle Christianity, Christ for All Nations, Jesus Image, Dunamis Movement, and many others, the aim of The Send is to get people involved in missions. I was really encouraged to see Carl Lenz, pastor of Hillsong New York, boldly representing Jesus in secular media in the United States and being a mentor to Justin Bieber in a way that has very publicly shown someone with huge influence starting to follow Jesus. I have also observed some great mission movements such as Josiah Venture creatively reaching high school kids in Europe or CV (Christian Vision) and Jesus.net making efforts to engage sharing the good news through technology and social media.

All this to say that there are lots of great initiatives happening around the world. There are numerous ways you can get involved. But most important, you can start where you are, with what you have. If you seek God with all your heart and obey his calling, you can be an instrument of change in His hands to reach this generation today.

If you want to get involved with Steiger, I encourage you to attend one of our training opportunities. Our main training is called the Steiger Mission School, which happens at our international centre in East Germany, near Dresden. Every year we have over twenty nationalities represented with a wide variety of gifting and background who feel called to join Steiger's mission to reach and disciple the Global Youth Culture for Jesus. The mission school combines three emphasis: seeking God through prayer and study of the Word in an undistracted environment, teaching and discussion on evangelism and discipleship to reach the Global Youth Culture, and powerful, engaging action as students participate in some of Steiger's front line missionary work. Find out more at www.steiger.org/sms.

Fighting the Good Fight

Anyone interested in getting involved in a movement like this will face serious challenges and opposition. It's the reality of the world in which we live—both the physical and spiritual world. If you are concerned about souls, you carry a spiritual burden. Anyone seriously sharing Jesus and praying for conversion and transformation will be entering a spiritual battle. The fight is real.

The morning of 13 May 2016 in Tübingen (Germany) I woke suddenly out of a dream. In the dream our team was standing by the tour vans after a concert when someone yelled, "there are lions coming!" I looked across the street and saw three lions prowling along the sidewalk. "Get in the vans!" I shouted. As we piled in the vans, the lions dashed at us. That's when I woke up. While on tour, we had been studying 1 Peter, so immediately a passage came to mind: "Be alert and sober minded. Your enemy the devil prowls around like a roaring lion looking for someone to devour" (1 Pet. 5:8).

As we met that morning with the team to pray, I shared the dream and said I thought God was reminding us of the spiritual battle we are in and that we should be alert and pray for protection. We prayed before we left for Zurich, Switzerland.

In Zurich we set up in a central square, but it was pouring down rain. A lot of people were out partying that night as the FCZ (Zurich football club) fans were celebrating a major victory. During our sound check, a bearded hooligan marched up to the stage and yelled that we had to cancel our show because they were having their party across the street. Our organiser explained that this fan club has one of the most violent hooligan gangs in Switzerland.

We played the concert in the pouring rain. Even so, around eighty people stood and watched the entire show. As I started the final lines of the show, going into the preaching, three angry hooligans stormed into the middle of the crowd. They were shouting and trying to spit at the band on the stage. One of them jumped at the front of the stage and punched my leg as I was preaching. Luke Wehr, our tour manager, tried bringing him to the side to talk, but the guy started swinging. A few security guys and members of the audience tried helping, and one young guy, who had been intently watching the show, got punched in the face. I asked everyone to calm down and said that I would no longer use the microphone from the stage: "If you want to meet Jesus tonight come to the side of the stage. The show is over". I hoped saying the show was over would satisfy the hooligans. I was wrong.

Off to the side of the stage our Swiss Steiger leader, Stephan, translated as I explained that we needed peace and that the only one who could give us peace was Jesus. Stephan also shared and then led people in a prayer to receive Jesus. While the hooligans marched about and were shouting, around twenty people stood in the pouring rain praying with us. One guy stood with tears streaming down his face while we spoke and then immediately left after the prayer. By the time we were done praying the three hooligans had left.

A security team member picked up a knife that one of the hooligans dropped in the struggle, making us deeply aware of the danger we were in. Stephan had called the police, but they were taking a while to show up.

The team started packing down the equipment. Suddenly a few hooligans turned up again and grabbed Stephan. A few of us ran over. As I walked toward the guy, I asked him to calm down. He reached into his pocket, pulled out some pepper spray, and hit me full on in the face with the liquid. My face and eyes felt like they were on fire, and I fell back choking. Before running off the guy also sprayed Yuki, our sound and stage manager, in the eyes. Ge Vang, one of our performers, and a few others chased the hooligans away.

I sat down trying to recover from the effects of the mace, and eventually the police arrived. Stephan and I went over to talk to them, but they just stayed in their vans and said to not worry. After around fifteen minutes they drove off. I told Stephan to call them back. I couldn't believe they just left us there. The team continued packing down the stage, but soon a group of hooligans started gathering around twenty meters from the stage. Before we knew it, there were about fifty of them huddled together as if planning an attack. I don't think I have ever felt so afraid. With incredible courage, the team continued packing down the stage. Yuki, still blinded by the mace, somehow continued locking down the stage trailer. I was trying to decide whether to tell our brave team to stop and flee to the vans or whether to try to get the stage and equipment out. Four police vans pulled up seconds before the mob was ready to attack. An outnumbered squad of around ten officers stepped out of their vans armed with riot gear.

Then the most amazing thing happened. The entire mob of hooligans marched across the square straight at us. I thought it was the end. I thought we were all going to get beaten up, and the equipment was going to get smashed. Miraculously the mob walked straight past us. They literally walked through the middle of our equipment and team and just kept walking to the other side of the square where the police were. Once they reached the other side, they attacked the police! The hooligans punched the police officers and took them down. They were rolling on the ground and punches were flying. It was a full-blown riot. We were in the middle of a war zone. From one side tear gas and rubber bullets were flying from the other flares, fireworks, rocks, and glass bottles. Our truck was hit a few times by bottles and Denny, our band pastor, was hit in the stomach by a rock. Tear gas canisters rolled around our vehicles as we frantically tried to hook up the stage trailer to leave.

After around ten of the most intense minutes of our lives, the whole team was in the vans and trucks and driving out of danger. At Stephan's house we joined together in the front room. Isaac, our drummer, said that the moment someone shouted "get in the vans" he immediately remembered the dream I shared that morning. We realised the miraculous protection of God that we had just experienced. Incredibly, no one was seriously harmed, and there was not a scratch on our equipment or vehicles. Watching a mob of hooligans walk straight through us reminded us of the angels of God closing the mouths of lions for Daniel in the Bible.

A Swiss news report came out the following day stating that a gang from FCZ attacked a Christian band and then the police. It also describes how after we left the gang gathered three hundred members to the streets to fight the police.

God had given us numerous warnings that danger was coming, but He also reminded us that He was in control and would protect us. David Pierce put out an incredibly prophetic post earlier in the day before all of this happened. It ended with this: "Whenever God moved in supernatural ways there was normally a riot that followed. Let the riots begin!!!"

In the face of spiritual battle, Peter instructs us to be self-controlled and alert. As missionaries in this secular age, in this intense and fast-moving Global Youth Culture, we need to be alert and aware of our purpose and what the cost is. It means sharing the spiritual burden of caring for people's souls. It means taking prayer seriously, both in your private life and as a community. I need a network of people praying for me, and I need to bring the team I work with together for regular prayer and encouragement in the Word. I need to ask God for his heart and guidance in every situation, that He would give me His perspective.

But being self-controlled and alert also means having my heart right before God and setting the right priorities: "It means holding ourselves to the highest priority year in and year out; not making our first priority to win souls, or to establish churches, or to have revivals, but seeking only 'to be well pleasing to Him'.... My worth to God publicly is measured by what I really am in my private life. It is my primary goal in life to please Him and to be acceptable to Him, or is it something less, no matter how lofty it may sound?"[1]

For a season in 2017 I felt called by God to step away from a project that was important to me so that I could prioritise caring for my family and spending time in prayer. On one hand, this is a difficult thing to do, but on the other, prioritising being with Jesus and caring for the family he gave me is the greatest joy I've ever known. I know that when He gives me the next challenge or when I face the next battle, I will only stand firm if my heart is right and pleasing to Him.

Our aim must be to please Jesus above all. Pleasing Jesus means knowing Him and having our hearts right before him. And in Him, we will have the strength to fight the good fight.

Something Worth More Than Life Itself

As I said in the introduction, my hope in writing this book was to raise awareness to the spiritual need of this Global Youth Culture and spark a mission movement where God might raise up hundreds of missionaries dedicated to preaching the gospel in cities across the world.

My prayer is that this book has somehow inspired you to follow wholeheartedly after the call of God on your life and to serve His mission today. We don't know how much time we still have left. This generation is lost and dying every day. They need to know the truth. The time to act is now.

I recently watched a documentary about the Maidan Revolution in Ukraine. The boldness and determination of the Ukrainian people fighting for their freedom is shocking. Many lost their lives defying the authorities and going against armed police battalions with sticks and stones. They fought for a political change and a temporal freedom.

We know the truth that can set all nations free and bring eternal hope for all humanity. For this we should be willing to lay everything down, with even greater boldness than those people at Maidan. We must be willing to lay down our comfort, our reputation, and our lives to share Jesus and the message of his death and resurrection for the salvation of all who believe.

This was the way the apostle Paul lived. He wrote a letter to a church he planted in Philippi while under house arrest in Rome. He and his team had been through a very intense time. It all started with a visit to Jerusalem, even though they had been warned it would be dangerous. Paul was arrested there and ended up on an unplanned long trip to Rome, during which he suffered assassination attempts, a ship wreck, and starvation. In all of this he did not give up but passionately continued to preach Jesus. In his letter, Paul declares that he is in chains not because of a crime he committed but because of his message about Jesus (Phil. 1:14).

In this dire situation, rather than complaining about hard times, Paul talked excitedly about the opportunity he had to witness to the roman guards, people in power in the palace, and even Caesar's own household. Paul was so passionate about his purpose and message, that this was all he thought of, even while in chains.

Paul's suffering led to unexpected fame. People pay more attention to you when you're willing to suffer for your message. But as always, fame brings jealousy. Other people who wanted to be famous like Paul started preaching the same message! Not because they wanted people to know Jesus but because they thought it would make them popular (Phil. 1:15-16).

Jealousy and criticism can sometimes be even harder than chains. When our reputation is on the line, we're tempted to give way and lose sight of our purpose. Paul did not lose sight. Rather than getting bitter, he rejoiced that the whole situation had brought attention to the message of Jesus (Phil. 1:18).

Preaching the cross will always mean stepping out and risking offence and losing friends. We need to be willing to walk through this so the message can be heard. Most of the time when people see you are genuine and real about the message, they are open. Paul was so passionate about his purpose and message, that he considered it more important than his own reputation.

Paul not only faced chains and criticism, but also the very real possibility of death. And it is in life-and-death situations that we think most deeply about our lives and our purpose. For Paul, even when facing the possibility of execution, he did not waver in his purpose and message. Instead he spoke even more boldly, in one of the most radical and beautiful verses of his letters: "For to me, to live is Christ, and to die is gain" (Phil. 1:21).

Paul found joy in life because his purpose is *the* purpose—to glorify his Creator, to spread the message of the love of God, to care for his brothers and sisters, and to change the world. He found joy in death because his purpose was eternal. His purpose was to know Jesus, which was complete when he died and went to be with Him. Paul was so passionate about his purpose and message, that he was willing to die for it.

He ended his letter by challenging the Philippians to have the same purpose and message, and to fight for it with the same passion. He wrote, "Whatever happens conduct yourselves in a worthy manner of the gospel of Christ" (Phil. 1:27), as if to say "you know the truth and you have the greatest purpose of all, to share that truth, so live in a way that shows that!"

That's my prayer. That we would use all our gifts and creativity, do the most unconventional things, and even risk our lives to reach the next generation. I pray that we would stand together with boldness to make the message of Jesus known today. So let's get out of the four walls of the church, off the coach, log off the news feed, hit the real world, and risk it all to reach the Global Youth Culture!

Appendix

Informal Bible Study Guide

What is an "Informal Bible study?"

The following material is taken from the "IsThereMore Informal Bible Study Guide," which I wrote for our mission Steiger.

The Global Youth Culture is one of the largest unreached cultures in the world today. Over the years Steiger has found creative ways to go to young people who would not usually walk into a church and relevantly communicate the message of Jesus. Many thousands have responded to this message, but one of the big challenges everywhere is how to offer a next step for these young people who have no church background and would generally struggle to connect immediately with a local church.

Once we've shared the gospel through an event or an ongoing relationship, it's important that we offer opportunities for people to learn more before they're ready to make a commitment. An informal Bible study is a great way for people to experience more of God and

His Word in a neutral and informal setting, whether they have already decided to follow Jesus or are simply interested in knowing more. It can also be a great way of starting a community in a place with no church.

Vision

An informal Bible study aims at offering community and contact with the Word of God as an immediate next step for those who have met Jesus at a show, event, or any other evangelistic opportunity offered by our missionary teams and are interested in knowing more. The goal is to form discipleship relationships with young people coming from a global and secular context, lead them into a strong and lasting personal relationship with Jesus, and help them get well connected with a local church community.

Audience

An informal Bible study should not be another meeting for Christians. The point is to create an environment where people who have never been to church feel welcome, where they can ask questions, say things you don't usually say in a church, disagree, and discuss relevant topics. If there are too many Christians in the meeting, they tend to dominate, answering all the questions and saying things that others don't understand. The Christians attending should be a select group who understand the vision and are there to support the leader and facilitate the meetings for those new believers or not yet believers. Other Christians who want to come should be lovingly encouraged to be part of their own local church and to not attend the meetings.

Informal Bible studies are catered to people who have possibly never read the Bible or been to a church. That means the leader needs to think about what he or she will say and how he or she will say it so that non-Christians can understand. It needs to be open and flexible to accommodate the flow of a community of new believers being formed.

To draw the right audience, the Bible study is designed to start in connection with an evangelistic impact opportunity like No Longer Music or a similar type of event relevant to the Global Youth Culture and that leads people to respond to the gospel message. At this evangelistic event those who respond or are interested in hearing more about the message are then invited to the Bible study. At the first meeting the full concept is presented so that people have the opportunity to commit to a longer period of meetings and gradually become part of a community.

Generally, to form an informal Bible study community with the right people it will take more than one evangelistic impact event. The team wanting to start a Bible study already should be actively involved in the local youth culture. This means regularly attending clubs, parties, and concerts so as to know the scene (see chapter 7) and build relationships. Once a few key influencers from a local youth scene attend, they often draw many others. For this reason an informal Bible study can work best when organised in partnership with the same young people you want to reach.

Location

Another important principle to make sure you draw the right audience is to pick the right location. An informal Bible study should happen in a popular venue that's easily accessible. It might be a café, a club, a cultural centre, a community house, or anywhere where people naturally gather. Sometimes it can help to start the Bible study in the same location where the initial evangelistic event occurred like a café on the square where a No Longer Music concert happened or even in the same club where the event happened.

Finding a neutral venue like this is important, as it can be challenging for people to walk into a church when the whole concept is new to them. The idea is to go to where people are and invite them into that informal and welcoming environment.

It is ideal to be able to create a good atmosphere and worth asking the owner of the café or club for permission first. If they don't like the idea of a Bible study in their venue, then any café or bar can work.

Asking some of the new participants, especially those well connected in the scene, for a place to meet can be really helpful to find the right place and also is a good way to encourage ownership with the participants.

Format

This guide presents content for fourteen weekly meetings: one intro party, eight Bible discussion meetings going through the Gospel of Luke, three topical meetings, one social event, and one baptism party. Alternate the types of meeting to keep them fresh and different each time.

Intro Party – This meeting should happen immediately after a band concert or any other evangelistic event, which is the best moment to invite people to an after party like this. It's an opportunity for people to meet, get to know each other, and hear stories. Ideally whoever made the invitation in the evangelistic event (the evangelist artist or speaker from the event) should be there to cast the vision for informal Bible study meetings. This is an invitation for people to join a mission to change the world by first changing ourselves through a relationship with Jesus. This first key speaker can share his story and why he follows Jesus.

8 Bible Discussions – The group discovers the truth of a Bible passage together through asking and answering good questions and seeking Jesus together in His Word. The leader assists the group in digging into the passage rather than only sharing his or her insights and answering the group's questions. It is important to let the people in the group discover for themselves the personality of Christ through studying the Bible. We want people to see His frankness, love, kindness, beauty, and, at the same time, His mysterious nature. Our goal is that people will experience the power of God's revelation through His Word. This will also inspire them to read and study the Bible personally at home.

3 Topical Meetings – In these we cover three basic discipleship topics: Bible, prayer, and the church. Here we can help uncover wrong perceptions about church, Jesus, faith, and other topics. The discussions should be creative, natural, and led in a way they understand.

1 Event – The objective with the event is to create an opportunity for those in the group to invite more of their friends. It is a chance to do something together and also a great evangelistic opportunity.

Baptism Party – This should be done at the church with the local church leadership. This is for those who choose to be baptised after going through the Bible study. In the topical meeting on community, one of the panel participants should explain baptism, that it is a confession of faith in Jesus to a community of believers that we become a part of.

Suggested Order

Week 1 - Intro party

Week 2 - The Jesus Revolution pt1

Week 3 - The Jesus Revolution pt2

Week 4 - Is the Bible a myth?

Week 5 - Something worth living for

Week 6 - God's broken heart

Week 7 - How can I pray?

Week 8 - Event

Week 9 - The ultimate life force

Week 10 - A great tragedy? pt1

Week 11 - A great tragedy? pt2

Week 12 - Power to raise the dead

Week 13 - Community: staying together

Week 14 - Baptism party

Getting Started

Get trained. The first step to lead an informal Bible study is to get trained. Steiger offers a two- to three-day in-person training, during which we cover the content of this guide and practically demonstrate the method. This training is also offered as part of the ten-week class at the Steiger Missions School in Germany. As part of this training in addition to the material in this guide you will need to read two books:

The Reason for God by Timothy Keller (Hodder & Stoughton, 2008)

The Bible Study Handbook by Lindsay Olesberg (InterVarsity Press, 2012)

Form a team and pray. Find a team of dedicated Christians who will partner with you in this vision. Meet for prayer and preparation every week and work together to build relationships with the youth in your community. Prayer is key. Pray for God to bring the right people and to have an impact on your city.

Organise an evangelistic impact event. This might be a concert, a party, an art exposition, or any event where the gospel can be shared and people can hear about the opportunity to be part of the Bible study. The first meeting should come as soon as possible after the main event that gets your informal Bible study started, and ideally the band, artist or key speaker from that event should be present.

Share what's happening. Promote your meetings through social media (start a Facebook page or group or Instagram account to share pictures and posts) and encourage participants to invite their friends. It is important to use marketing tools to promote the Bible study. Choose a name for your meetings and ask a designer to help create a logo or some visuals and promotional material to get the word out. Think of concepts that will communicate well with your audience. For example, in the Russian speaking world, Nuteki created the concept #6PMBible that was branded simply as café, youth, Bible. The Steiger Brazil team advertises their group as a Bible study for the non-religious.

Think of something that fits your context. Feel free to ask other Steiger leaders for help in this.

Bible

One of the main emphasis in an informal Bible study is helping people who have never walked into a church have contact with the Word of God and meet Him as He powerfully reveals himself through the stories and lessons of Scripture.

Lindsay Olesberg explains how "most of us tend to pay more attention to the words of experts than to the words of the Bible itself".[1] She reminds us about the Bereans who were commended for:

> That very night the believers sent Paul and Silas off to Beroea; and when they arrived, they went to the Jewish synagogue. Now the Berean Jews were of more noble character than those in Thessalonica, for they received the message with great eagerness and examined the Scriptures every day to see if what Paul said was true. (Acts 17:10-11)

The Bereans are called more noble than the Thessalonicans because they were interested in the message and then turned to examine Scripture to see if it was true. For them the Scriptures were central. This is a great way to study the Bible and the Global Youth Culture really identifies with figuring things out for themselves. In a time of scepticism toward institutions and authorities, young people today are not inclined to just sit and listen to a leader explain what they should believe. For a generation that is used to finding their own answers and making their own decisions, the concept of discovering the answers for themselves really resonates with them.

Putting the Bible at the centre is the basis for Olesberg's method to Bible study. She believes that anyone can come to it and observe, question, discover, learn, and ultimately meet God. Her method of study follows three basic convictions:

Facts before theories. Often we come to the Bible with our own assumptions and ideas of what it should say. Then we try to validate those assumptions by finding things in the Bible that confirm our ideas. The danger here is that often our ideas may not be completely accurate. By studying and teaching the Bible this way, to an extent we can make the Bible say what we want it to.

The scientific world describes two approaches to exploring and learning: deduction and induction. Deduction is when we use what we already believe to be true to study and understand reality. Induction is when we explore reality and allow it to teach us what is true.

For the informal Bible study we use the inductive method to study the Bible. As Olesberg says, it is the spiritual discipline of putting facts before theories. We should approach the Bible as the Word of God and true authority in our lives, and therefore make it central. We come to it without assuming we already know what it says, and we allow it to teach us. This is very helpful when reading the Bible with people who have never read it before. As Christians, when we read the Bible our heads are often full of explanations we've heard before. Unbelievers don't have that history. They are coming to the passage fresh with no idea what it says or means. By asking questions we discover together what it means, rather than assuming we already know.

Author determines meaning. One danger in coming to the passage as a group of unbelievers who are open to discovering what it says is that we can get all kinds of interpretations. We allow the pluralistic and relativistic context of our Global Culture to lead us to a subjective discussion where our own opinions of what it says becomes central rather than the Bible itself.

Olesberg gives us an important principle to follow to avoid this. The basic point here is that *we* don't determine the meaning, rather we should look at the context of the writing and the author's intentions to understand the meaning. It means seeking to understand what the author wanted his original audience to understand, rather than what it means to us in our day and age.

Understanding requires application. Following the first two principals means we will have a good understanding of the Bible passage and what it means, but it is only when we choose to believe, allow it to sink into our hearts, and then apply it to our lives that we are truly meeting Jesus. It is through this principle that discipleship truly begins to happen.

Therefore, as we study and discover God's Word together, it is essential we ask questions not only to understand the passage also our assumptions, beliefs, and selves. These Bible discussions should include questions and points that help us understand how to apply what we've learned in a practical way to our lives.

Community

Running an informal Bible study is primarily about two things: meeting Jesus and creating a community.

When we gather together, with the Scripture at the centre of our communal life, something beautiful develops. Studying the Bible in community grounds us, feeds us, weaves us together, and launches us out into the world to take our part in God's mission.

In this sense we realise that the church, this family that Jesus established, is what this generation is looking for. But often the gap between the church and the outside world hinders the sense of community. This is where an informal Bible study can bridge the gap.

This is an opportunity for community and contact with the Word of God to happen before someone is ready to walk into a church. For that reason it is very important that the team leading the group to create an environment that encourages genuine community. These are a few practical points that can help in forming a healthy community around the Word:

Welcome newcomers. An informal Bible study should be primarily focused on new people joining. It should not become another church meeting or a closed club. As you lead think about what it would feel like for someone who has never been to a church or a meeting like this. Would they understand what is being said? Would the place and atmosphere seem familiar and welcoming? Would they feel part of the group or like an outsider? Put yourself in the place of a newcomer and seek to develop an atmosphere that welcomes and helps people feel part of the group.

Everyone's contribution is important. The Bible studies and topical meetings should be an open discussion, welcoming and valuing everyone's contribution. Having a mixed group of mostly non-believers means that people may often say things you don't agree with or feel are off topic. But it is essential to listen to and value every contribution. A good discussion facilitator will know how to interact with everything shared in the discussion, remembering themes and questions members bring up and drawing the more introvert people into the discussion.

Time together. The meeting is not just about the Bible study or discussion. Community can happen only if you allow the group to enjoy spending time together. The informal settings help with this, but it is important that in every meeting the group can enjoy spending time together. For this to truly happen, the community you are forming has to become more than the meetings themselves. The relationships should develop into something deeper than a weekly meeting. You should welcome people into your life, to your home to share a meal or to go out together.

Leading and caring for people. The team leading the Bible study should be regularly praying for each person who turns up at the group. It is our responsibility to care for the spiritual growth of those who have come seeking to know Jesus. The leaders should be spending time listening to their stories and seeking ways to care for and guide the people as they discover what it means to follow Jesus. This is all part of the discipleship process.

Purpose and action. Life in community must lead to action. Bonhoeffer explains that community gives the person the opportunity to put faith into practice by sharing it with others. Getting young people practically involved in the kingdom plays a powerful role in discipleship. In finding acceptance, truth, and identity, we also find the passion to be involved in changing the World around us. The best remedy for a disconnected consumerist society is to be involved in social transformation, sharing the good news, and making disciples.

Young people today can be the best agents of change and trendsetters in a globalised society, front-liners in the spreading of the kingdom in a fast-changing world.

Bible Study Meetings

Preparing

As I mentioned above we follow Lindsay Olesberg's "communal discovery" method of Bible study where the group discovers the truth of a Bible passage together through asking and answering good questions and seeking Jesus together in His Word. The leader assists the group in digging into the passage rather than only the leader sharing insights and answering the group's questions.

We use what's called the manuscript format when reading Bible passages. There are no verse numbers, chapter divisions, headings, or notes at the bottom of the page. This format helps the participants see the passage in a way that's familiar to them.

Each communal discovery Bible study starts with a few minutes of personal time for the group to read and mark their texts. The group spends the rest of the hour sharing what they see in the text, sharing questions that arise from the text, and grappling with those questions as a group. The leader helps summarise the main points or flow of the passage. Finally, the group discusses how the passage relates to them and how they could apply it. The leader's role is to facilitate the discussion and the discovery process.

As the leader study the passage first before leading the group. As you study each passage, make sure you make a personal application to your life. What is Jesus saying to you in each passage and calling you to do or change? Study the passage first, apply it in your life, then lead the group. In this way the passage will have gripped your own heart and life, and you can teach it with real power and conviction.

Preparation Step by Step

This material goes through the Gospel of Luke, so the first thing you want to do is read through the whole book and study it inductively. As you read, pray that God would reveal himself to you and think about the following questions:

What is the context? (place, time, issues, author, readers)

What is the writer's purpose?

What is the order in the book?

What are some of the themes? Is there a main theme?

After making your own notes on the book, have a look at what some of the Bible commentaries say about Luke. Most study Bibles have commentaries; you can also find various options of commentaries online or to order from book shops.

After this background preparation, you are ready to study each specific passage that the group will focus on in the meetings. Study the passages like this:

Facts. What does the passage actually say? What are the facts?

> Read the passage carefully and write down specifics that you see, such as who is there, what is happening, when is it happening.

Circle or write down similar or contrasting words, phrases, or ideas or ideas that go from the general to the particular or state a cause and effect.

Put yourself in the passage. If it is a narrative, put yourself into the story. What do you see, smell, taste, and feel? Choose one of the characters and become them.

Meaning: What does it mean? What did the author intend it to mean?

What questions does the passage raise in your mind? What words, phrases, or concepts don't you understand? Does the passage turn in any unexpected ways? What intrigues you? Write these things down.

Application: What is God saying to me and how will I put this into practise in my life?

Step back and read the passage a few more times. Ponder again the points that stand out to you in the passage. What does the passage say or point to about Jesus?

As you ponder your study, do you sense that God is speaking to any part of your life? Is there a promise to trust, a command to obey, or an example to follow or avoid? Is there a deeper insight into God or your experience with God? What action are you going to take in response to what God is saying to you?

Summarise

Write down the key thoughts and questions that came up under each step (facts, meaning, and application). Identify the main points of this passage. Develop four or five questions that can help the group come to their own understanding of the passage and the main points you identified.

This guide already presents an introduction and questions for each passage, but it is important that you do your own personal study of the passage to be ready for the meeting. You can use your own questions instead of or in addition to the ones in this material, and ultimately it is the themes and questions that the group bring up that will be your most valuable material to lead the discussion.

Leading the Discussion

Don't talk too much, don't preach, don't lecture, and don't share everything you prepared. Get the group to share what they see in the passage. Have the group itself generate the questions, and then dig together for answers.

When you feel it's time to ask one of the prepared questions, wait for people to answer. Listen to their answers and ask more to get them talking, and be flexible, be willing to talk about what they bring up. Always stop and ask if they have questions. At the end, conclude clearly. Tell personal stories to give examples.

General Outline of the Meeting

Free time (10 min)

Allow free time at the beginning for talking, snacks and drinks, and whatnot.

Introduction (15 min)

Have a dynamic creative start to catch everyone's attention. If possible, have a band play a couple of songs and the leader presenting the theme. This should be more like an acoustic show style, or lounge music, not worship music. (It's not a church service).

Read the passage out loud (5 min)

Group exploring (30 min)

Share your observations and questions together. Help the group by asking questions like What caught your attention? How would you describe what is happening? What did you understand about this passage? What else did you notice? Make sure you are asking open-ended questions and not obvious content questions like Who did Jesus encounter on the road to Samaria? Don't answer the questions yet, this is a brainstorming time, it should be lively and dynamic, with everyone sharing thoughts and questions.

Walk through the passage using the key questions that the group identified. Use the questions in the informal Bible study material or your own questions when necessary to cover the key sections of the text. Encourage the group to seek answers in the passage.

Summary and application (10 min)

After walking through the passage and answering the questions as a group, a few main themes should emerge. Summarise those in a few sentences. Ask one or two questions that encourages personal application. End with the key application points, challenging the group to put what they have heard into practice. The informal Bible study material includes applications and conclusions at the end to help end the meeting with a clear and powerful message.

Prayer (10 min)

End with a prayer. Ask if anyone needs prayer. This can be a really powerful time, especially for people who have not prayed much before. If you have the right audience (non-believers) they will not be comfortable to pray themselves yet, so you should pray for them.

Free time (10 min)

End again with free time for talking, more snacks and drinks, and whatnot.

Total time: 1h30min

Topical meetings

Preparing

Invite three people to participate in a panel on the topic. Ask the panellists to watch the Steiger video about the topic (Bible, prayer or community found on the website www.istheremore.info), and prepare some thoughts, questions, and personal testimonies related to the topic. For instance, on the topic of prayer panellists can share what prayer means to them personally, a story about answered prayer, or situations that helped them understand prayer better.

Panellists can also find a few Bible passages and quotes or examples from pop culture or writers that relate to the topic. Panellists can share their thoughts with each other before the meeting to think about ways to interact with each other.

Free time (10 min)

Allow free time at the beginning for talking, snacks and drinks, and whatnot.

Introduction (20 min)

Have a dynamic creative start to catch everyone's attention. If possible, have a band play a couple of songs and the leader presenting the theme for the meeting. This should be more like an acoustic show style, or lounge music, not worship music. (It's not a church service).

Watch the Steiger video at istheremore.info (5 min)

Panelists share some thoughts (15 min)

Each panellist can have five minutes to share their prepared examples and insights on the topic.

Questions (20 min)

Let the group ask questions or make comments on what the panellists shared. The panellists can also interact with each other, asking questions or commenting.

Summary and application (10 min)

Summarise the key points, conclusions, or outstanding questions. Choose a key insight you feel would help the group with their questions and struggles and end by emphasising that insight and suggesting a practical application.

Prayer (10 min)

End with a prayer. Ask if anyone needs prayer. This can be a really powerful time, especially for people who have not prayed much before. If you have the right audience (non-believers) they will not be comfortable to pray themselves yet, so you should pray for them.

Free time (10 min)

End again with free time for talking, more snacks and drinks, and whatnot.

Total time: 1h40min

Event

An informal Bible study should be outward focused, always open and welcoming to new people. While it is focused on introducing those new or not-yet-believers to the faith and the Bible, it should also be seen as an ongoing evangelistic opportunity. A newcomer arriving at any meeting should be able to join in and feel part of the discussion.

An event is a great way to keep the Bible study dynamic and outward focused. It should be organised by the group together, and the leader should seek to include the participants in the action. Discuss with the group ideas of what kind of event to organise, where to do it, and how to invite new people.

We suggest the event be creative and artistic. It can be a film discussion, an art exhibition, a series of workshops, a music concert, or any number of things. Partnering with non-Christian artists is a great way to draw new people. For example, if your group wants to host a music concert, invite a few well-known local bands who can draw an audience, and one Christian band who can share a message. Building relationships in the scene is very important and should be an ongoing effort of the team. Inviting local artists and getting to know them and their audience is a good way to do this.

It is really important to take the opportunity to share a clear gospel message again in this event. If there aren't any Christian bands or artists able to share a clear message, maybe one of the informal Bible study organisers can do this. If the event is a film discussion, choose a film that can lead to a good discussion and a gospel presentation. If it is an art exhibition, seek an artist who can share his faith through the art and/or through an interview at the exhibition. After sharing the message, you can invite people to the Bible study that will continue the following week.

Make sure the promotion for the event is visually attractive, done with relevant language and branding, aiming for high quality design and concept. Get the whole group to share with all their friends and find ways to do the event in the scene and in a location that connects with the scene like a coffee shop or club.

Baptism

Churches and denominations do baptism differently, so it is important to discuss this with your local church (if there is one) and decide together how to welcome these new believers and baptise them. It's important to do the baptism with the local church.

It is very important to invite people to be baptised once they've had the chance to understand who Jesus is and have chosen to believe and follow Him.

In the topical meeting on community, one of the panel participants should explain baptism, that it is a confession of faith in Jesus to a community of believers of which we become a part. It's also important to remind participants about what they have learned through the Bible study and to make sure they understand what they are confessing in the baptism: repentance and faith in Jesus as Lord and saviour.

The baptism, a party celebrating new life and a welcoming into the community of faith, is a great way to end this important time. We pray you would see many people meeting Jesus and being baptised in the informal Bible study!

Sample Bible Studies

You can request a full Informal Bible Study guide at www.steiger.org

You can also find more Bible studies at www.istheremore.info

The Jesus Revolution pt1

Introduction

Welcome to [name of your Bible study]. This is only the beginning. We believe this time here together can change everything. We want to change the world, but we believe this starts inside each of us. The revolution has to begin inside our own hearts.

Share a personal story about a key moment in which Jesus became real to you.

If you are here it's because you believe there is more to life than what we see around us and what society and the media tells us. You probably heard our message in our show. I don't know what your thoughts are on God and religion. I don't know if you believe in something like that or not. But if you're here I imagine you are at least curious.

Our goal here is to explore the big questions in life, those questions we often think have no answers. We want to hear your thoughts and we want to discover answers together.

We believe God is real and that he is here in this room right now. You are not an accident; you were created by a loving God who knows you and cares about you. We believe that we can know him by getting to know Jesus. So we want to read the story about Jesus found in the Bible.

Jesus was and is a revolutionary, but unlike other revolutionaries in history who tried to change the system, Jesus' revolution begins inside the human heart.

In the passage we read today Jesus walks into a religious meeting and is invited to read from an ancient Jewish prophecy. As he reads, his voice is so full of power and authority that everyone's eyes are fixed on him. The prophecy describes this moment of hope, when everything would change, something everyone present hoped and believed would happen someday. Jesus puts down the scroll and says "this is happening right here and right now..."

Read: Luke 4:14-22

Questions

What can we find out about Jesus in this passage? Who was he and what was he like?

It says he was brought up in Nazareth. What do you think that would have been like talking to a crowd that has known you since you were a child?

Jesus seems to be declaring his life mission. What is it? How would you describe it?

What do you think the prophecy meant by the poor, prisoners, blind, and oppressed? Do you think it is literal or figurative?

What did Jesus mean by saying, "Today this scripture is fulfilled in your hearing?"

Summary and application

Do you think people today in our society ever feel poor, broken-hearted, captive, blind, or oppressed? Do you ever feel this way? Do you think Jesus is able to fulfil this mission of setting the captives free, healing and bringing sight to the blind today?

Jesus came for the poor, broken-hearted, captive, blind, and oppressed. Most people in that time felt like that. They were oppressed by the Roman Empire and many were waiting for a political leader to come and free them and change the system – but Jesus didn't do that.

Today people feel poor, like something is always missing; captive by the system, a job, social pressures, drugs, addictions, bad relationships, materialism, the list is endless; oppressed by what harm may be doing to them or by remorse for harm they have caused to others; blind and yet knowing there is truth somewhere out there but never finding answers.

But often the type of freedom we're looking for is not the freedom we really need. We want to change the world around us, the system or our circumstances, but what we really need is a change of heart. Jesus' revolution starts inside our hearts. He wants to set us free inside. He wants to heal our broken hearts and he wants to help us see the truth.

Ending prayer

The Jesus Revolution pt2

Introduction

Welcome back! If you were here last time, we are really excited that you are here again. If this is your first time, then you are very welcome here too.

Last week we started by reading a passage in the book of Luke, which is part of the Bible. We were trying to understand who Jesus is. We talked about how Jesus was a revolutionary but that he was a different type of revolutionary. His revolution starts in the human heart; it changes us from the inside out.

Share a personal story about how something significant changed in your life as you started to follow Jesus.

The passage we will read today tells the story of a guy willing to do anything to find change. This guy was a real fighter who didn't accept things the way they were. He was tired of his life the way it was. He wanted to be healed and changed. That's why he went looking for Jesus. But when he found Jesus, the change Jesus brought took him by surprise and went beyond what he expected.

Read Luke 5:17-25

Questions

This is a crazy story! Where did these guys come up with the idea of climbing on the roof with a paralytic man and make a hole to lower him down?! Put yourself in the place of the paralytic man. How do you feel? What are you thinking? What are you expecting?

What did Jesus mean by "your sins are forgiven you"? And why did he start by saying that instead of healing the man? Why were the religious people angry?

Putting yourself in the place of the paralytic man again, what are you thinking and how are you feeling now after receiving what Jesus had to offer?

Summary and application

What is this forgiveness of sins, and is it something we still need today? Is there such a thing as sin?

Last week we saw how Jesus came to set the captives free, heal the broken-hearted, and give sight to the blind. We discussed about whether this was literal or figurative, relating to states of the soul. We saw today that Jesus seems to be offering both physical and spiritual healing – freedom in the body and in the soul.

Jesus wants to give us forgiveness, an inner freedom. This is freedom from our corrupt nature and our pride. Interestingly the paralytic man wasn't really looking for that. He hoped for physical healing, but Jesus' first concern was with his heart not his legs.

Jesus is a revolutionary who came to set us free, but we need to understand what he is freeing us from. This revolution starts within – in our character and in our hearts. Maybe we're looking for a lot of things in this life, but when we find Jesus, we discover what we really need is this inner change, forgiveness of our sins.

The religious leaders were angry because they had power over religious ceremonies like offering forgiveness of sins. They ran a complex and lucrative system of animal sacrifice in the temple to declare people free of sin. Jesus bypasses the system and offers forgiveness free of charge. That is because there is a power in Jesus that cannot be found in any religion. Jesus defeated death, so he can defeat the death that is inside of us. It is his gift to us.

Ending prayer

Something Worth Living For

Introduction

Sometimes when touring with our band we go through some tense moments, often real danger.

Tell a story about being attacked and facing opposition.

I believe this happens because God has called us to have a radical faith, a faith we will fight for and risk our lives for, one that will cost us everything.

Often today it seems like we've lost our passion for life. There seems to be nothing really precious in life, nothing really worth fighting or dying for. We've become so comfortable. But in Jesus we can find our passion again. Here is something worth dying for.

Following Jesus comes at a cost. It means dying to myself, humbling myself before God and saying, "God I need you; I need you to change me". It means complete surrender.

The story we will read today is about a guy who had this kind of radical faith. He was willing to give up everything to follow Jesus.

Read Luke 5:27-32

Questions

Who was Levi?

What can we learn from this passage about how tax collectors were seen in Jesus' time?

What were the costs and consequences for Levi to follow Jesus?

Why were the religious people angry with Jesus?

How does Jesus define his mission in this passage?

Summary and application

Why do you think Jesus compared sin to being sick? What does this comparison say about sin? According to Jesus, what is the cure?

Jesus seems to be suggesting that everyone has this sickness and needs this cure? Do you agree? Is this true today?

When we decide to follow Jesus, the first thing he wants to do is that inner revolution we talked about in the last study. We are all sick, and he has come to heal us. This cure comes through repentance, which means to ask God for forgiveness and to surrender everything to Jesus in a radical step of faith with suicidal tendencies.

Ending prayer

God's Broken Heart

Introduction

Share a personal story of love for a family member – child, spouse, sibling, or parent.

Last week we talked about this radical faith and about surrendering everything to God. But who really is this God we are giving up everything to follow? What is he like? Does he really care about me and my life?

Often when we think of God we think of an old man in the sky, someone far away, or we think of the paintings or stained-glass windows of a church. But God is not a distant being waiting to punish us when we make a mistake. He is here right now in this room. The Bible describes him as a loving father. Not an alcoholic father or a violent father, like we may experience in this world, but a perfect loving father.

Jesus told a story to help us understand God's heart for us. We're going to read that today.

Read Luke 15:11-24

Questions

Let's first put ourselves in the place of the father. How did he feel when his son asked for his inheritance and left? Did the father do the right thing in letting him go? What would you do?

What is the son like, what attitudes did he show?

Put yourself in the place of the son at the moment he decides to return home. What is he feeling? Why does he want to return? Why does he feel he has to offer himself as a servant to his father?

What is the father like? What attitudes and character can we see in the passage?

Who do you think the father and the son represent? Some have said they represent God and humanity. Do you agree with this?

Summary and application

If this story represents God and us, what does it say about our condition before God? What do we need to do about it?

The story began with a son thinking of himself, wanting to be free of his obligations and of the influence of his father. The story ends with the son returning home, loved, accepted and restored. Maybe the most important discovery we make today is about God's attitude towards us, his lost sons and daughters: God's heart is broken for the lost. He is a loving father who patiently awaits our return. This story shows us how Jesus saw the situation between us and God, and it gives us hope: God will forgive those who choose to follow the example of the lost son, who repented and returned home.

About Steiger International

Join us!

Steiger International is a rapidly growing worldwide mission organization that is called to reach and disciple the Global Youth Culture for Jesus.

Steiger raises up missionaries and equips the local church to proclaim the message of Jesus in the language of the Global Youth Culture and establishes long-term teams in cities through creative evangelism, relevant discipleship, and local church partnerships.

For more information on Steiger and how you can get involved, go to **www.steiger.org**.

Steiger Missions School

If you feel called to join Steiger International, the first step is to attend the Steiger Missions School (SMS). This school takes place twice a year at our International Centre in Krögis, Germany, and lasts for ten weeks.

The SMS is intended for people with a wide variety of gifts and backgrounds who feel called to join Steiger's mission to reach and disciple the Global Youth Culture for Jesus.

For more information and to apply for the missions school, go to **www.steiger.org/sms**.

Global Youth Summit

Join church and missions leaders, and young people from Europe and beyond, to tackle the

question of how to reach the Global Youth Culture for Jesus.

Steiger's annual festival-style conference is sure to inspire, energise, and equip you.

www.steiger.org/globalyouthsummit

Come&Live!

Come&Live! is a worldwide community of artists who are boldly using their God-given talents to share the revolutionary message of Jesus with those outside the church.

For more information on Come&Live! and how you can get involved, go to **www.comeandlive.com**.

This author is also a regular participant in our weekly podcast called *Provoke & Inspire*.

About the Author

Currently, Luke is living in Wroclaw, Poland, with his wife Ania and their two children. He regularly organises protests with his "riot rock" band The Unrest and serves as the European director for Steiger, a mission organisation dedicated to reaching and discipling the Global Youth Culture for Jesus.

Luke's passion is in evangelism and discipleship among the alternative scenes of the Global Youth Culture. In previous years, Luke worked with Steiger Brazil, guiding a Brazilian version of the band, No Longer Music; the community house "Espaco Coletivo"; and a movement of evangelistic art and music events called Manifeste.

In more recent years Luke has helped establish Steiger teams in Poland, Germany, Finland, Portugal, Ukraine, Belarus, and Russia. His vision for Steiger in Europe is to see Jesus proclaimed to young people all over the continent. He wants to establish dynamic missionary teams reaching the Global Youth Culture and developing ongoing discipleship relationships and local church partnership, in every key urban centre.

In addition to such projects, Luke often speaks around the globe, sharing the vision of Steiger in churches and conferences, as well as teaching each year at the Steiger Missions School on the topics of Evangelism and Discipleship in the Global Youth Culture. He challenges people to live a radical faith and courageously engage the Global Youth Culture with the Gospel.

To invite Luke to speak write to **europe@steiger.org.**

Check out Luke's current band The Unrest on social media platforms **@theofficialunrest.**

Notes

Introduction

[1] Pew Research Center, "America's Changing Religious Landscape," March 12, 2015, https://www.pewforum.org/2015/05/12/americas-changing-religious-landscape/.

[2] Harriet Sherwood, "'Christianity as default is gone': the rise of a non-Christian Europe," March, 20 2018, *Guardian*, https://www.theguardian.com/world/2018/mar/21/christianity-non-christian-europe-young-people-survey-religion.

Chapter 1: Unhappy, Unloved, and Out of Control

[1] Catherine Mayer, "Unhappy, Unloved and Out of Control". *Time*, April 7, 2008, 35-40.

Chapter 2: The Calling

[1] For more information read *Rock Priest* by David Pierce (1998).

Chapter 3: The Largest Unreached Culture Today

[1] Aleks Krotoski, "Youth culture: teenage kicks in the digital age," Guardian, 25 Jun 2011, https://www.theguardian.com/technology/2011/jun/26/untangling-web-krotoski-youth-culture.

[2] "Teens, Social Media & Technology," 2018, 31 May 2018, Pew Research, http://www.pewinternet.org/2018/05/31/teens-social-media-technology-2018/.

[3] "More and more young adults addicted to social media," Center for Big Statistics, 18 May 2018, https://www.cbs.nl/en-gb/news/2018/20/more-and-more-young-adults-addicted-to-social-media.

[4] Alison Battisby, "The Latest UK Social Media Statistics for 2018,"

Avocado Social, 2 Apr, 2018, https://www.avocadosocial.com/the-latest-uk-social-media-statistics-for-2018/.

5   Stuart Dredge, "42% of people using dating app Tinder already have a partner, claims report," Guardian, 7 May 2015, https://www.theguardian.com/technology/2015/may/07/dating-app-tinder-married-relationship.

6   Brian Peters, "Top 10 Powerful Moments That Shaped Social Media History Over the Last 20 Years," Buffer, 30 Jun 2017, https://blog.bufferapp.com/social-media-history.

7   Ndasauka Y, Hou J, Wang Y, Yang L et al. (2016) Excessive use of Twitter among college students in the UK: Validation of the Microblog Excessive Use Scale and relationship to social interaction and loneliness. Computers in Human Behavior, 55, 963-971.

8   Graham C.L. Davey Ph.D., "Social Media, Loneliness, and Anxiety in Young People" Psychology Today, 15 Dec 2016, https://www.psychologytoday.com/us/blog/why-we-worry/201612/social-media-loneliness-and-anxiety-in-young-people.

9   Sabrina Barr, "Six ways social media negatively affects your mental health," Independent, 28 Jan 2019, https://www.independent.co.uk/life-style/health-and-families/social-media-mental-health-negative-effects-depression-anxiety-addiction-memory-a8307196.html.

10   Zymunt Bauman, *Globalization: The Human Consequences*, Cambridge: Polity Press, 1998.

11   Andrea Smith, "We're travelling even more than ever, according to the World Tourism Organisation," Lonely Planet, 19 Jan 2017, https://www.lonelyplanet.com/news/2017/01/19/travelling-world-tourism-organisation/.

12   Amanda Machado, "How Millennials Are Changing Travel," Atlantic, 18 Jun 2014, https://www.theatlantic.com/international/archive/2014/06/how-millennials-are-changing-international-travel/373007/.

13   Zymunt Bauman, *Globalization: The Human Consequences*, Cambridge: Polity Press, 1998, 79.

14   Dossiê universo jovem 4 MTV, 2008, Production: MTV Brasil.

15   Zymunt Bauman, *Globalization: The Human Consequences*, Cambridge: Polity Press, 1998, 80.

16   Ibid., 48.

17   Proven Men Porn Survey (conducted by Barna Group), 2014, https://www.provenmen.org/2014PornSurvey/.

18   Social Media Addiction – Statistics and Trends, Go-Globe, 26 Dec 2104,http://www.go-globe.com/blog/social-media-addiction/.

19   "Alarming Video Game Addiction Statistics," http://www.addictions.com/video-games/alarming-video-game-addiction-statistics/.

Chapter 4: What You Believe Matters

[1] James W. Sire, *The Universe Next Door: A Basic Worldview Catalog*, 4th ed., (Downers Grove, IL: Inter Varsity Press, 2004), 17.

[2] Paul Kurtz and Edwin H. Wilson. "Humanist Manifesto II". *American Humanist Association*, 1973, http://americanhumanist.org/Humanism/Humanist_Manifesto_II.

[3] Francis A. Schaeffer, *The God Who Is There* (Downers Grove, IL: Inter Varsity Press, 1968), 5.

[4] Ibid., 17.

[5] C. S. Lewis, *The Abolition of Man* (New York: Macmillan, 1947), 91.

[6] John Lennon, 1965 interview.

[7] British Humanist Association, "What Makes Something Right Or Wrong? narrated by Stephen Fry, 17 March 2014, https://humanism.org.uk/thatshumanism/.

[8] Timothy Keller, *The Reason for God* (New York: Viking, 2008), 9.

[9] Terry Eagleton, *The Meaning of Life* (Oxford: Oxford University Press), 2007, 66, 62.

Chapter 5: Lost

[1] Lead singer of Blur, quoted in Graham Cray, *Postmodern Culture and Youth Discipleship* (Cambridge: Grove Books,1998), 12.

[2] Florence Welch of Florence and the Machine in a 2018 interview for Universal Music about her new album *High as Hope*, https://www.youtube.com/watch?v=WhwJAuRsntg.

[3] Ibid.

[4] Bryn Phillips, "The 2011 riots taught us nothing: when will the young and dispossessed kick off again?" *Guardian*, March 10, 2016, https://www.theguardian.com/commentisfree/2016/mar/10/2011-riots-england-uprising-working-class.

[5] Jonathan Watts, "Brazil erupts in protest: more than a million on the streets," Guardian, 21 Jun 2014,

https://www.theguardian.com/world/2013/jun/21/brazil-police-crowds-rio-protest.

[6] Paul Danahar, *The New Middle East*, paperback edition (New York: Bloomsbury, 2015), 278.

[7] Mary O'Hara, "Young people's mental health is a 'worsening crisis'. Action is needed," *Guardian*, 31 Jul 2018, https://www.theguardian.com/society/2018/jul/31/young-people-mental-health-crisis-uk-us-suicide.

[8] Suicide data, World Health Organization, Mental Health Action Plan, 2013-2020, http://www.who.int/mental_health/prevention/suicide/suicideprevent/en/.

Chapter 6: The Source of Hope

[1] "68% of the world population projected to live in urban areas by 2050, says UN," 16 May 2018, https://www.un.org/development/desa/en/news/population/2018-revision-of-world-urbanization-prospects.html.

[2] Greater Europe Mission website, http://www.gemission.org/mission-and-vision.

[3] Howard Taylor, *Hudson Taylor's Spiritual Secret* (Chicago: Moody Publishers, 2009), 32.

Chapter 7: Know the Scene

[1] David Bivin, "Rabbinic Parables," Judaic-Christian Studies no. 5, https://www.cfi.org.uk/downloads/rabbinic-parables.pdf.

Chapter 8: Speak the Truth

[1] Francis A. Schaeffer, *The God Who Is There* (Downers Grove, IL: InterVarsity Press, 1968), 123, 127, 129.

[2] Bonhoeffer, *The Cost of Discipleship*, 30

Chapter 9: Stay Together

[1] Bonhoeffer, *The Cost of Discipleship*, 48

[2] Augusto Cury, *O Futuro da Humanidade*, (Editora Arqueiro, 2005), 85 (my own translation).

[3] Bonhoeffer, *Life Together* (London: SCM Press,1954), 8.

[4] Lindsay Olesberg, *The Bible Study Handbook* (Downers Grove, IL: IVP Connect, 2012), 85.

Chapter 10: Join the Revolution

[1] Oswald Chambers, My utmost for His highest.

Appendix: Informal Bible Study

[1] Lindsay Olesberg, *The Bible Study Handbook* (Chicago, IL: InterVarsity Press, 2012), 30.

44092637R00122

Printed in Poland
by Amazon Fulfillment
Poland Sp. z o.o., Wrocław